Backstage Economies

Labour and Masculinities in Contemporary European Dance

Backstage Economies

Labour and Masculinities in Contemporary European Dance

Dunja Njaradi

University of Chester Press

First published 2014
by University of Chester Press
University of Chester
Parkgate Road
Chester CH1 4BJ

Printed and bound in the UK by the
LIS Print Unit
University of Chester
Cover designed by the
LIS Graphics Team
University of Chester

© Dunja Njaradi, 2014
Photographs
© Kerem Sanliman, 2008
© Max Moser, 2003

All Rights Reserved
No part of this publication may be reproduced, stored in a retrieval system or transmitted in any form or by any means without the prior permission of the copyright owner, other than as permitted by current UK copyright legislation or under the terms and conditions of a recognised copyright licensing scheme

A catalogue record for this book is available from the British Library

ISBN 978-1-908258-14-4

CONTENTS

Acknowledgements	vii
List of Illustrations	viii

Chapter One
What is Dance? An Introduction to 'Contemporary Dance'
1. Introduction — 1
2. Writing Dance History: Dance and Modernity — 10
3. Writing Dance History: Postmodern Dance and Beyond — 22
4. Globalization, Hybridity, and Contemporary Dance — 38

Chapter Two
Shattered and Sown Europe: Theoretical Questions and Methodological Approaches to Study Dance under Globalization
1. End of the Cold War and Cultural Policies in Europe — 51
2. Contemporary Dance in South East Europe — 61
3. Methodology — 67
4. Dance and Gender — 73
5. Dance as Labour and Production — 79

Chapter Three
Gender and Masculinities in the World of Contemporary Professional Dance
1. Introduction — 91
2. Gender in the History of Western Theatrical Dance — 93

v

3. Dancing at the Borders of Europe: Ziya Azazi — 100
4. Doing Dance in Postsocialism: 'Alexander', 'Peter', and Igor — 107
5. Concluding Remarks — 122

Chapter Four
Dance Performance as Labour and Production
1. Introduction — 132
2. Immaterial Labour and Dance in South East Europe — 134
3. Dance Performance as Production: From Marx to Virno — 143
4. Creative Work Against Body Work: Changing Economies of Dance Labour — 151
5. Dancers Speak of Ballet, Contemporary Dance, and Work — 155
6. Conclusion — 164

Chapter Five
Conclusion
1. A Few More Words On: Contemporary Dance and Global Mobility — Routes Versus Roots — 171
2. 'Backstage Economies' and New Dance Methodologies — 180
3. Postscript: Belgrade 2013 — 186

Bibliography — 192

Index — 218

ACKNOWLEDGEMENTS

This book is a result of the generosity of many people and institutions, and I wish to thank them all here.

I wish to say a big thank you to the Theatre Department of Lancaster University for support during the initial phase of this long-term research. The Department of Performing Arts at the University of Chester gave me precious time and support to turn this research into a book. I am especially grateful to Professor Darren Sproston and Sarah Griffiths for their steady support.

This book would not exist without the dancers who were generous in giving me their time in the midst of their exceedingly busy schedules and I have had nothing but enjoyment from being immersed in their lives and work. I am especially grateful to Ziya Azazi and Igor Koruga, the dancers and my dear friends.

This book is dedicated to my mother — she taught me to work hard.

LIST OF ILLUSTRATIONS

Front Cover Image
Ziya Azazi in *Dervish* by Kerem Sanliman (Istanbul, 2008).

Back Cover Image
Ziya Azazi in *Dervish in Progress* by Max Moser (Vienna, 2003).

Colour Plates

Plate 1: Ziya Azazi in *Dervish* by Kerem Sanliman (Istanbul, 2008).	127
Plate 2: Ziya Azazi in *Dervish* by Kerem Sanliman (Istanbul, 2008).	128
Plate 3: Ziya Azazi in Dervish by Kerem Sanliman (Istanbul, 2008).	129
Plate 4: Ziya Azazi with the author in Budapest in 2008.	129
Plate 5: Igor Koruga in *Come Quickly, My Happiness is at Stake* (2012).	130
Plate 6: Igor Koruga in *Temporaris*, a co-authored performance (2011–13).	130
Plate 7: Igor Koruga in *The Scale* (2011) with Josephine Larson Olin.	131

CHAPTER ONE
WHAT IS DANCE? AN INTRODUCTION TO 'CONTEMPORARY DANCE'

1. Introduction

> I am Saša Asentić, native of Bosnia and Herzegovina, based in Serbia. This was 'My Private Bio-Politics' performance.
> After the premiere the most important question to me was: why did festivals from Western Europe such as Tanz-im-August (TIA) invite me to perform?
> I asked myself the question because I couldn't understand it – this work criticizes a Western monopoly over contemporary dance; besides it is neither Balkan-exotic nor virtuous; moreover it is not even a dance.
> So, why have I been invited? (Asentić and Vujanović, 2008:78)

This after-performance statement of Serbian dancer and performer Saša Asentić summarizes some of the basic challenges set by the contemporary processes of the unification and creation of the common European culture. These processes include significant negotiations between the national (local) and the transnational (global) within the boundaries of the nation state (Boon and Delanty, 2007). They also create a new social reality, a reality which is 'by no means a purely normative idea based on various abstract ideals but is, rather, empirically situated in the here and now — while making reference to that which is beyond the local, national or even European level' (ibid.:31).

Asentić's dilemma indicates what has been deemed one of the most important features of these processes that shape the new social reality of Europe: 'the way the West perceives the East [and the way] the East looks at how the West views the East' (Levy and Sznaider, 2007:171). Asentić, thus, begs an important question about the cultural appropriation of differences within Europe and ways of criticizing the global from the position of the local, nation-state, position.

This book will investigate contemporary dance and globalization in multicultural and cosmopolitan Europe, relying on the investigation of living and working patterns of four male dancers. It will use methodologies developed within both anthropology and dance studies. It will explore memories (of socialism), new art and dance practices, and new labour and living patterns of global citizens. As a result, it will adopt theoretical and methodological tools developed within anthropology and dance studies to challenge the boundaries of both disciplines.

Choosing dancers for the focus of the book has several important consequences. Given the nature of their work, especially given the recent changes in the regime of work (Bauer, 2008; Kunst, 2010a), dancers represent paradigmatic examples of highly mobile global citizens. Further, the affective and embodied 'work' of dance can shed some light on the embodied aspects of participation (within ethnic, national or global communities). In Judith Hamera's words, dance technique: 'recreates neighbourhoods as sites of productive, diverse allegiances. It transforms the sparseness of studios into home places and bodies into maps. It organizes relationships across culture and class to form affective environments, geographies of the heart' (Hamera, 2007:60).

Lastly and more specifically, in South East Europe as the place of origin of three of my dance subjects, dancers and artists had a crucial role in creating and developing the so-called third-sector practices and agencies. Third-sector practices and agencies are situated in non-governmental and non-commercial realms and can refer to activities and services from social and health care to various cultural and educational programmes. Thus the third-sector came to be the supplier of services from which the welfare state is progressively withdrawing (Böse, Busch, and Dragićević Šešić, 2006:132). The investigation of the third-sector became increasingly important in understanding complexities of South East European transition since its significance grew in both the 'transitional societies' of Eastern Europe and in neo-liberal economies. It is also crucial for understanding Eastern European dance scenes that were developing with significant support from the third-sector agencies and this will be explored further in the book.

The ethnographic method, which this thesis employs, recently gained significant attention in dance studies (Banes, 1994; Grau, 1994; Martin, 1992; Desmond, 2000). Jane Desmond, discussing new tendencies within dance studies, proposes 'terra incognita' (Desmond, 2000) as a term to mark ethnographies as a possible solution to the problems dance scholars face. She argues that dance scholars should 'expand [their] methods of analysis to include more ethnographies of institutions and audiences' (ibid.:43). Desmond's critique of existing dance scholarship relies on the idea that dance scholarship lately has suffered from 'too much' of a cultural studies approach, shown to be limited in terms of its capacity adequately to embrace and explain the 'phenomenon' of dance.

Although acknowledging the benefits of feminist and poststructural approaches to dance scholarship, Desmond at the same time is critical of cultural studies scholars who 'sometimes draw selectively on certain anthropological texts (by authors such as James Clifford, Clifford Geertz, and

George Marcus), but [when] in practice there is relatively little cooperation with those whose primary training prepares for fieldwork rather than textual analysis' (Desmond, 2000:44). Therefore, what Desmond further explains is that dance scholars who adopt ethnography as a primary methodological focus are pushed to the margins and are 'not read and cited widely by dance scholars beyond the context of the "dance ethnography" world' (ibid.:44). The 'worlds' of dance ethnography and dance studies appear either side of a binary divide.

This book, although trying to bridge this gap, is not, however, strictly anthropological in the sense that it does not rely on a dedicated and long-term research relationship with a certain place (locality) and culture (often identified with the place in question), which has traditionally been the focus of anthropological studies (Gupta and Ferguson, 1992). This books pays more attention to the condition of ethnography under globalization that profoundly questions the significance of place (locality) and puts more emphasis on global networks. Unlike some globalization theorists, however, such as Castells (1996), who claims that in the condition of globalization the 'space of flows' superseded previous 'space of places', I will follow Gille and Ó Riain's belief that 'we must develop our understanding of how places and networks constitute one another, rather seeing them as opposing principles of social life' (Gille and Ó Riain, 2002:275). This book, thus, is not ethnography, but combines the efforts of both dance studies and anthropology to view their respective methodologies critically and to address the phenomenon of dance in globalization.

Addressing the phenomenon of dance, from whichever methodological standpoint, is not an easy endeavour because its seminal term, dance, is so hard to pin down.

What is Dance?

Questions that come immediately to mind, for instance, are—What sort of dancing? What is dance? Are we speaking about theatrical dance, folk and social dance, or about various movement forms that occur during ritual and trance? Anthropologists were traditionally interested in the latter, writing about social, folk, and ritual dances, whereas dance studies busied itself with developing methodologies to address dance as art and not as social practice. This division, of course, started to blur with the poststructuralist project to undermine Western philosophical assumptions and values (Rowell, 2009:139), when the focus in dance studies shifted away from seeing dance as art, to an over-reliance on social and cultural contexts.

This book employs dance studies and anthropological methods to observe contemporary Western theatrical dance. This means that it will look at cultural, historical, and economic contexts including close (field)work with selected dance practitioners. It will examine theatrical (not usually conceived as ethnic) dance which is the focus of dance studies but will also explore cultural and racial differences as dance anthropologists often do.

Working with dancers and including their personal stories and histories in scholarly volumes has become more of an acknowledged method in dance studies (Shay and Fisher, 2009; Risner, 2009). This shift owes much to 'reception-based criticism that values the case history method' (Shay and Fisher, 2009:6), but also to some ground breaking research in dance education that shifted scholarly attention to a dancer's experiences in education and training (Risner, 2009). For this book, I worked closely with four selected male dancers and interviewed numerous other dancers, dance producers, and managers. The research is not meant to offer an educational corrective to dance training or to the phenomenological enquiry into the experience of dance, but it is meant to address anthropology as an 'equal partner' in exploring the phenomenon of contemporary dance in Europe.

This research took place, with different intensities, between 2008 and 2013. Throughout 2008 and 2009, I travelled to Turkey, Romania, Serbia, and Macedonia where I met and worked with my dancers. Our meetings also took place in France, Austria, and the United Kingdom because the life of a dancer is always on the move. My dancers are Ziya Azazi, an Arab Austrian born and raised in Turkey; Igor Koruga, living and working in Serbia and Germany; 'Peter' from Romania, and 'Alexander' from Macedonia. Some of the artists presented here are nationally and internationally known professionals. Others are, or were, semi-professional or more aligned with pedagogy or cultural management. In some cases I have used pseudonyms which are designated by the quotation marks. All of the artists whose real names appear here, and whose words constitute the core of this project, gave permission to use real names. The fact that they are male dancers allowed me to address dance and masculinity—that 'elephant in the room' (Shay and Fisher, 2009:5) of dance studies. Their personal stories and histories reveal much about dance and gender—unveiling different and opposing understandings of dance practices and dance aesthetics, and their living and working patterns provide an important analytical window to address contemporary lives under globalization. Therefore, the fact that they come from specific geopolitical locations will also be explored in much detail throughout this book. That said, whereas their gender is the same, everything else including their age, dance practices and aesthetics, sexual preferences etc., is different.

What is Dance?

This book intersects these stories and histories within a specific geopolitical location—that of South East Europe. Therefore, some attention should be given to the history of anthropology connected with this region. For instance, Katherine Verdery, one of the most prominent anthropologists of socialist and postsocialist Eastern Europe, recollects how in the early seventies when she was a graduate student about to choose her fieldwork, 'Eastern Europe was less known to anthropology than was New Guinea' (Verdery, 1996:5). This was due to the specific understanding of the 'Otherness' in the anthropology of that time (where white European societies were not strictly understood to be 'different') and also to the nature of the Cold War politics where Eastern Europe was simply out of reach. Soon, however, Verdery discovered her own academic capital in choosing to investigate Eastern Europe: her work might not have been prestigious but it was bound to be 'pioneering'. Although Verdery's account testifies to all sorts of practical issues relating to the choice of fieldwork an anthropologist might face, it is not without the traditional anthropological colonial investment in the exotic and dangerous. Thus, Verdery adds:

> To allure of this professional kind one might add the romantic aura, the hint of danger, adventure, and the forbidden, that clung to the Iron Curtain and infused the numerous spy stories about those who penetrated it. To go behind the Iron Curtain would be to enter a heart of darkness different from that of Conrad's Africa or Malinowski's Melanesia, but a darkness nonetheless. (Verdery, 1996:5–6)

Given the fact that Eastern Europe, although significantly under-researched in the history of anthropology, had a status of 'darkness nonetheless' during the Cold War and before (see Wolff, 1994), it is important to revisit its status after the Cold War with the process of European integration. In a sense, it became obvious that European integration brought about a certain disintegration of Eastern Europe: some Eastern European countries were 'granted' a part in the 'family' of Europe, whereas some (most notably South East European countries) were not. This calls into question not only the notion of Eastern Europe but also demands much more attention to be paid to the very notion of 'difference' in a globalized world. Throughout my research, I was frequently forced to question my own geopolitical location as I struggled to obtain relevant visas to travel to Western Europe and I was surprised and moved by the occasional moments of cultural intimacy (Herzfeld, 2005) with my dancers. Moreover and more generally I was constantly confronted with my own efforts and inability to both understand the 'Other' (anthropological effort) and to write (about) dance performance (the most urgent question of dance methodology).

However, this research does not address dance performances as such. As my research progressed, I gradually became more interested in writing about dance environments or dance lives in the globalized Europe, rather than dance performance as an event. In October 2009, I was visiting a dancer in Montpellier where the prestigious programme 'Six Months, One Location', organized by Xavier Le Roy and Bojana Cvejić, was taking place. I visited a dancer who was taking part in this programme and we were sitting in the communal kitchen where the dancers were in the process of preparing their evening meals and seemingly relaxing. Dancers were talking among themselves, and the conversation revolved around jobs/money/projects with a gentle gossip about people in the field and the so-called 'star figures'. Some of the present dancers, I learned later, were also PhD students. The way these dancers talked about what they do and what seemed important (and what bothers them as well) corresponds to Paolo Virno's writings on the subjectivities in contemporary labour regimes which now employ 'fundamental abilities of human being ... with language, thought, self-reflection and the ability to learn' (Virno, 2003). I soon learned that these dancers are extremely articulate about what they do, about projects they are pursuing. In these conversations, the word 'choreography' was almost obsolete and the understandings of what constitutes the work and world of contemporary dance were diverse. In a way, this situation is not exclusive to the world of dance. John Roberts in his brilliant study on deskilling in arts after the readymade, discusses a figure of a contemporary artist which he terms a post–Cartesian artist which 'is not a name for a particular kind of artist or even a particular kind of artistic virtue, but, rather, convenient shorthand for a number of different social and cultural tendencies which have gathered force since the first two decades of the twentieth century' (Roberts, 2007:102).

Contemporary dancers are affected in the same way with a plethora of social and cultural tendencies and above all with dramatic changes in a wider economy. Dance 'skill' is no longer defined by what the body can do, but by the way this body interconnects with other bodies and spaces and this is where the importance of the dance labour should be discussed.

This book frames these questions through the discussion of contemporary dance under globalization using personal narratives and recollections of my dancers. The following three sections will address these questions under the subsections of: a) dance history (writing) through the discussion of relationship between dance, language, and modernity; b) dance and 'contemporary condition of modernity' through the discussion of modernism and postmodernism in dance (analysis); and c) dance and globalization.

2. Writing Dance History: Dance and Modernity

During the last thirty years anthropology has made some significant endeavours to overcome the radical dichotomy between knowledge and praxis/agency, through the decentralization of the cognitive construction of knowledge (in poststructuralist terminology, between text and event). As a result of these efforts, many new conceptual approaches to questions of the body have been born. Thus, 'body is no longer seen as a model of social organization, nor as a biological "black box", cut off from the mind' (Lock, 1993:136), and interpretations based on the annihilation of the metaphysical mind/body dichotomy have become theoretically and scientifically privileged. This conceptual change in understanding the body reflects theoretical changes in anthropology and other social sciences under the influence of poststructuralism and feminism (Thomas, 2003; Shilling, 2004). Other domains of science, such as the various domains of cognitive science and philosophical approaches based on phenomenology, have also devoted special attention to and raised significant interest in the ways in which the specific nature of human embodiment contextualizes and makes a contribution to our mental states and properties (Clark, 2008). Dance studies seemed to fall outside his general shift in social sciences (Farnell, 1994; Desmond, 1993; Koritz, 1996). Brenda Farnell in her 'Ethno-

What is Dance?

Graphics and the Moving Body', argues that there is a fundamental problem with Western ways of viewing human movement. She suggests that despite an upsurge of interest in 'the body', an understanding of a person as a moving agent is still absent from cultural theory and ethnographic accounts (Farnell, 1994). Jane Desmond traces this 'turn to the body' in the social sciences with the advent of cultural studies, concluding, much in line with Farnell, that this critical work focused on the representation of the body rather than on bodily movement/actions. To Desmond this 'academy's aversion to the material body, and its fictive separation of mental and physical production, has rendered humanities scholarship that investigates the mute dancing body nearly invisible' (Desmond, 1993:34).

Although I am not entirely convinced that there is a prevailing aversion in the social sciences regarding the materiality of the body, it certainly seems to be the case that the phenomenon of the body and the moving body is neglected in social sciences.

The second interrelated problem that dance studies faces is the almost ontological condition of dance: dance vanishes — 'It doesn't "stay around" (for such is the unfortunate condition of its materiality)' (Lepecki, 2004a:130). The ephemeral nature of dance performance is one of the oldest and most pressing questions for the whole project of dance theory (Noverre, 1983; Siegel, 1972; Lepecki, 2004b, Franko, 1995; Sparshott, 1982; Carter, 2004a; Thomas, 2004; Foster, 1996a). Marcia Siegel summarizes this issue as follows:

> People are thrilled by it because it is so singular an occurrence. When you have seen a dance, you've done something no one else will do again. But for this very reason scholars can't get hold of it. Dance leaves them with

nothing tangible to analyze or categorize or put on reserve in the library. (Siegel, 1972:xiii)

Marcia Siegel further claims that dance's ephemerality is often mistaken for triviality and is the reason for the relatively subordinate position of dance within the system of art, and, I would add, for the underdevelopment of dance studies. Indeed as early as 1760, one of the first dance critics, writer and choreographer Jean-Georges Noverre cried: 'Why are the names of maîtres de ballet unknown to us? It is because works of this kind endure only for a moment and are forgotten almost as soon as the impressions they had produced' (Noverre, 1760, cited in Copeland and Cohen, 1983:10).

One of the ways of capturing dance's ephemerality throughout dance history (in order for dance to have a history) is through writing and seeing dance as a written text. Mark Franko in *Dance as Text: Ideologies of the Baroque Body*, claims that 'At the dawn of theatrical dance in France, choreography was frequently likened to, and indeed contrived to suggest, a written text' (Franko, 1993:15). The other, more recent, but interconnected ways of 'capturing' and historicizing dance is through extensive documentation, preservation and reconstruction of dances especially of the early American modern dance era (Thomas, 2004:32). Of course, seeing dance or a dancing body as a text has historical repercussions and dynamics within histories of dance theory. Here I am thinking about specific post-structuralist approaches to dance that re-emerged in dance studies, albeit from different theoretical, historical and political standpoints. Dance writings such as criticism, notation and autobiographies are one way of documenting/ preserving dance history. Seeing dance as a text, from whichever historico-theoretical standpoint is one way of understanding/analyzing dances in their historical contexts.

The second possible way of thinking about dance history is through the development and succession of dance technique. According to the prominent early twentieth-century critic, John Martin, with the succession of Romantic ballet the technique ceased to be 'supplementary reinforcement to (the dancer's) art … it is the dance itself' (Martin, 1980:302). What Martin implies is that only with the 'victory' of ballet's 'pure' technique in the nineteenth-century Romantic ballet, did ballet finally become an art in itself detached from opera, pantomime, and acting. To understand the change Martin implies it is helpful if we look at, for example, Noverre's eighteenth-century understanding of ballet. Noverre divided dance into technique (what he calls mechanical or technical dancing)[1] and the artistic component (what he calls pantomime and narrative dancing) (in Franko, 1993:146). Needless to say Noverre places much more emphasis on the artistic component to define 'good' ballet. Although the question of the artistic and technical components of dance is far from being resolved as Martin implies, there are good reasons to pay attention to dance technique.

First of all, the development of dance technique could provide analytical lenses to look at gender, and the social and cultural circumstances of a given historical epoch. However, technique is also a live and physical signature passed from a dance master to pupil and consequently 'rewrite[s] bodies' and communities' relationship to space and time, and to the intersections of both' (Hamera, 2007:60).

---

[1] Actually, Noverre calls technical dancers 'machine men' which will be of importance in further discussion.

Dance technique also delineates dance from other socially constructed movements of the body. Randy Martin observes that:

> Technique can be viewed as producing both the dancer's means of sustenance and the basis of exchange, both among other dancers and between culture and polity. ... Technique is the means through which the raw kinetic materials of dance are transformed into movement which have identifiable and repeatable value within dance. (Martin, 1990:112)

There are several means by which we can observe the development of dance technique. First of all, unlike dancers from previous decades who were usually educated exclusively in one technique (ballet, Graham, Cunningham, and others), contemporary dancers are encouraged to train their bodies in as many techniques as possible in what Susan Foster calls the phenomenon of the 'hired body'. To Foster, this eclectically trained dancer as a 'hired body' is shaped by economic forces and lacks depth and specific artistic vision (Foster, 1997). I will not take issue with the implication of this statement regarding the artistic lack of the 'hired body', but draw attention (as Foster rightfully does) to the idea that technique and training patterns are shaped also by economic imperatives.

The dancers I have been working with are certainly good examples of this phenomenon. Only one of them, 'Peter', has a formal ballet education (although he also received training in a variety of contemporary techniques as well). All of my dancers were exposed to a number of different techniques and styles. None of them, apart from 'Peter', has a formal dance education.

What is Dance?

The second important issue related to dance technique is that historically it seems that technique is getting more and more technical, i.e. acrobatic (Gard, 2006; Wainwright and Turner, 2004). As one dancer[2] recently observed:

> Technical levels have improved dramatically around the world ... when you have someone like Sylvie Guillem [Principal dancer of the Royal Ballet], who has that kind of body [almost skeletally thin and incredibly flexible] you wonder where one day it's going to stop. I just wonder how much you can push their bodies to the limits. The thing is bodies have changed dramatically over the years ... I think as dance goes it's like an evolution of mankind. Bodies will change to adapt to do better and better things. It's much more athletic than it was 20 years ago. (cited in Wainwright and Turner, 2004:325)

This quotation opens up some important questions. Generally, it points to the way in which the body has historically been invaded and transformed by subjective definitions that accord with particular sociocultural values and aspirations. More specifically, it points to the way we might think about the relationship between dancing bodies and the development of (bio)technologies (De Spain, 2000), a question that seems to be gaining in urgency. Increasing technical demands on dance bodies, however, can be also seen as inherent in the internal development of ballet technique. Hammond and Hammond (1979) observe ballet history from the perspective of development of its technique. They claim that the development of technique has less to do

---

[2] An anonymous dancer of the English Royal Ballet who took part in Wainwright and Turner's research (2004) on ballet body and injury.

with talented individuals (famous ballet masters) who had been 'inventing' new and daring steps, but instead, in Weberian fashion, they emphasize the accumulative character of technical development—changes are only imaginable and new possibilities arise only from within existing technical conventions. Hammond and Hammond's research is significant as they emphasize ballet's technical history and occurring changes as twofold—both influenced by external social, cultural, and political factors and deeply rooted in already existing technical traditions and pasts.

For the moment, however, I wish to return to the question of the ephemerality of dance. As already discussed, dance's vanishing nature is also connected to its alleged triviality in comparison to other arts. However, this 'negative' side of dance also has been seen as a specific 'power' of dance. One of the fervent believers that dance and text are interchangeable, Jean-Georges Noverre, was also among the first to realize that there is an excessive aspect of dance which cannot be fully grasped in writing nor fixed by notation. More recently, André Lepecki observed that:

> In other venues ... ephemerality that represented a deadlock for dance studies for so long proved to be dance's most powerful weapon. Franko observes that under the influence of deconstruction 'dance's self-erasure has been ... reformulated as a powerful trope for new theoretical (as well as performative) interventions in dance, and in writings on dance, beyond the documental tradition'. (Lepecki, 2004a:131)

The writings of dance scholars influenced by poststructuralism and deconstruction emphasized the liberatory potential of dancing bodies whose materiality and kinaesthesia are able to escape the overarching workings of language and signification. Further to this, with the advancement of modern dance technique in the early twentieth century, the ephemeral nature of dance increasingly came to be seen as an advantage. Andrew Hewitt asserts that:

> The fact that dance does not produce a 'work' or artifact to mark the fact that work had taken place particularly suited it to an aesthetic ideology of modernism that sought to obscure the materiality of work in its own productions. There is a fantasy of pure energy at play here that parallels a capitalist fantasy of pure profit, pure production. (Hewitt, 2005:26)

What Hewitt underlines is that in the twentieth century, with the advancement of modern dance, the kinaesthetic potential of dance—the fact that it provides communication with no recourse to language—is seen as a perfect form of immanent democracy. In this light Hewitt makes a useful comparison between ballet and modern dance bodies by which 'Ballet arose from a fantasy of absolute control (articulated as visibility, the opening up and splaying of the dancer's body for surveillance)' whereas modern dance 'envisages a social order in which such control is superfluous because each individual has an immediate, fundamental, grounding relation to the whole' (ibid.:29). This celebration of pure energy is, however, entirely consistent with the modernist vision of capitalism that also conceptualized the human body and labour in energetic terms.

Let us briefly look at the social origin of change in the conception of the human body that also resulted in changes to the dancing body during industrialization and modernization. The much acclaimed work of Michel Foucault explores the relations between power and knowledge in discourses of modern societies. Foucault's critical focus is precisely on regulation of and control over the human body and sexuality throughout eighteenth-century Europe. Foucault argues how throughout the eighteenth century there was a significant change in the relationship between individual and political power (both in terms of societal institutions and more sophisticated and implicit discursive systems), which resulted in the shift from the spectacle of torture to the modern disciplinary regime. This new modern system depicts power whose function is to create 'a certain mode of detailed political investment in the body, a "new microphysics of power"' (Foucault, 1991:139). Susan Foster similarly notes that during the 1700s and early 1800s 'scientific enquiry into the bodily origins of human identity moved incrementally forward ... scientists linked both emotional responses and predispositions to precise physical mechanisms' (Foster, 1996b:151). Although both Foucault and Foster root this change in a certain 'medicalization' of the body with the advancement of medicine and human sciences, I propose that this change is rooted in the advancement of industrialization and the move from a matter-based physics to an energy-based model. According to Anson Rabinbach (1992), the great discoveries of nineteenth-century physics led to the reconceptualization of the human body as a thermodynamic machine[3] regulated by 'internal dynamic principles, converting fuel into heat, and heat into mechanical work' (ibid.:52; see also Armstrong, 1998; Wendling, 2009). This machine-man concept emerged significantly in the nineteenth century, with industrial societies

---

[3] First law of thermodynamics: energy is at a constant level in the universe, it cannot be created or destroyed; it merely changes form.

relying on advances in human sciences and technology (Comacchio, 1998). Correspondingly, human labour was also 'cleansed' from its social, cultural, and moral dimensions — 'work can be reduced to an amount of heat or motion performed' (Rabinbach, 1992:73).

Thus, this 'energistic model' (Wendling, 2009) of the interaction between humans and nature likened human embodiment to mechanical embodiment, with human labour described in terms of energetic conversion. Wendling especially emphasizes that Karl Marx was influenced by this model when introducing the term labour power into his theoretical writings. Thus 'Labor power — comes to distinguish the quantifiably measurable units of force added by workers to production, and the quantifiably measurable units of force needed to supply workers with the basic life necessities (e.g. food, sleep)' (ibid.:83).

The theoretical and philosophical implications of Marx's conceptions of labour power and body-as-machine had a profound influence on modern dance.[4] Felicia McCarren asserts that 'The redefinition and abstraction of labor in terms of energy, movement, muscle, and rhythm, in the application of thermodynamics of working bodies, reveals the profound sociocultural implications of work-science and suggests a common culture linking dance to machine' (McCarren, 2003:19). Similarly, Norman Bryson notes the correspondence between the analysis of human movement and the Western vision of industrial movement by claiming that 'The meshing together of economic and kinetic abstraction in industrialization represents, in anthropological terms,

---

[4] For the connections between repetitive, machine labour and dance in both the industrial and the post-industrial workplace, see Radcliffe and Angliss (2012).

an epochal change in the history of socially structured movement and in the human object world' (Bryson, 1997:71). Thus, we can trace how the body as machine had a particular root in capitalist modernity but also how that same modernity seeks to recover 'primordial' and 'natural' conditions of mankind.[5] Oskar Schlemmer, father of the 'mechanic ballet' in the early twentieth century, summarized this tension in the art of his time as follows:

> Life has become so mechanized, thanks to machines and a technology which our senses cannot possibly ignore, that we are intensely aware of man as a machine and the body as a mechanism ... modern artists long to recover the original primordial impulses; on the one hand they woke up to the unconscious, unanalysable elements in the art forms of non-intellectuals: the Africans, peasants, children, and madmen; on the other hand, they have recovered the opposite extreme in the new mathematics of relativity. Both these modes of consciousness — the sense of man as a machine, and insight into the deepest wells of creativity — are symptoms of one and the same yearning. (Schlemmer, 1990:126-7)

Schlemmer's quote is a paradigmatic example of what Fredric Jameson (1979) calls the aspirations of high modernism. These tried to resist the commodity form as embodied in mass culture, i.e. to clearly delineate elite art from the mass culture which became increasingly entangled under the condition of fast industrialization and mass production. This

---

[5] This tension also haunts Marx's own writings on labour and labour power as a difference in new thermodynamical conception of work and the older Hegelian ontological notion of work that emphasized work as self-creating and spiritual expression of human beings (for discussion see Wendling, 2009).

What is Dance?

aspect of modernist thought which emphasizes the tensions between progress based on technological advances and yearnings for the lost primordial past gave special shape to the modern dance aesthetic and technique (McCarren, 2003). I would like to add however that even ballet technique, which is usually seen as the antithesis of modern dance technique, originates from this impetus. This does not only mean that eighteenth- and nineteenth-century ballet masters employed the metaphor of the machine or imagined corps-de-ballet as the machine, although these concerns were not entirely foreign to them,[6] but that the praxis of the persuasive remodelling and reshaping of the living materiality of the human body through the advent of rigorous ballet technique made the living machine-man possible. What I am saying here is that the fact that dance is primarily a praxis is its primal political significance. As Andrew Hewitt emphasized:

> dance [can serve] as the aesthetic medium that most consistently [seeks] to understand art as something immanently political: that is, as something that derives its political significance from its own status as praxis rather than from its adherence to a logically prior political ideology located elsewhere, outside art. (Hewitt, 2005:6)

This quotation does not, however, imply that we should abandon looking at ideologies that surround and contextualize diverse dance practices. If the long-term

---

[6] 'Dancing Masters frequently referred to the body as the human machine and believed that their pedagogical strategies effectively calibrated and aligned its workings. Like Pygmalion's statue, the body could be made to come to life and move beautifully if the proper care were taken' (Foster, 1996b:69).

engagement with the social nature of the body across cultural studies and humanities can teach us something, it is that careful historical and geopolitical contextualizations are always necessary in understanding the political immanence of any praxis.

I will, therefore, in the following section open up a discussion on the historical context of my research and analysis by examining the modern/postmodern debate in art and humanities. This debate is important for dance studies as they struggle to identify modernism and postmodernism in dance and thus consolidate theoretical and analytical approaches to study dance historically. Lastly, this debate is crucial in discussing the narratives of my dancers as the end of postmodernism is frequently equated with the end of the Cold War which, on one hand, brought about a certain erasure of Eastern Europe through the politics of European integration and, on the other, strengthened the notion of Eastern European 'difference'.

3. Writing Dance History: Postmodern Dance and Beyond

Examining the nature and diversity of the broad movements in culture known as 'modernism' and 'postmodernism', Malcolm Bradbury states that the fall of the Berlin Wall in November 1989 was a powerful moment in history born out of the conviction that we are entering 'a fresh phase in the human story' (Bradbury, 1995:763; Birringer, 2003; Forrester, Zaborovska and Gapova, 2004; Chioni Moore, 2001). This belief was strongly felt not only in the realm of geopolitics but in the diverse realms of art and culture (Bradbury 1995). To Bradbury, this rapture marks the end of postmodernism in culture and arts, because soon it became obvious that 'this was no End of History but a return to history' (ibid.) and this

What is Dance?

realization became an important element in artistic expressions, as well as in cultural and geopolitical debates. Bradbury identifies postmodernism in arts and culture with strategies of pluralism, parody, and quotation followed by the disappearance of traditional cultural hierarchies. At the same time, he underlines that: 'What was taken away from the cultural centre was, admittedly, often restored at the cultural fringes: political writing was granted to the repressed cultures of eastern Europe, to post-colonial societies, to emergent ethnicities, but not to dominant centres' (ibid.:770).

According to Bradbury, two 'problems' emerged regarding this after the end of the Cold War. The first is closely connected to the fact that '"post-modernism" had long since ceased to be a style, an aesthetic or metaphysic [but] it had become a fate or a general condition' (ibid.). This is exemplified in the writings of Fredric Jameson (1991), for whom 'postmodernism' refers to the cultural logic of late capitalism. In relation to postmodernism and art Jameson, for instance, asserts that:

> the new political art—if it is indeed possible at all—will have to hold to the truth of postmodernism, that is to say, to its fundamental project—the world space of international capital—at the same time at which it achieves a breakthrough to some yet unimaginable new mode of representing this last, in which we may again begin to grasp our positioning as individual and collective subjects and regain a capacity to act and struggle which is at present neutralized by our spatial as well as our social confusion. (Jameson, 1994:25)

Jameson identifies the theory of postmodernism as one that affirms gradual homogenization between economic and cultural levels so that the previous belief that artistic engagement escapes the reaches of commodity form does not hold true (Jameson, 1998). Hal Foster clarifies this stance:

> A fundamental aspect of postmodern culture may be the collapse of the distinction between the economic and cultural realms, the breakdown of the old structural opposition of the cultural and economic in the simultaneous 'commodification' of the former and the 'symbolization' of the latter. (Foster, 1985, cited in Auslander, 1992:10)

Moreover, Jean Baudrillard (1981), among others, claims that in postmodern culture we have to account for an entirely new symbolic order by which the excess of signs and of meaning in late twentieth-century 'global' society had caused (quite paradoxically) an effacement of reality. In this conception, globalization is equal to postmodernism as a highly mediated society of mass communication.

Postmodernism is, thus, applied to a whole host of movements, many in art, music, and literature, that reacted against a range of tendencies in the imperialist phase of capitalism called 'modernism'. Since the term gained currency far beyond the domains of arts and culture, the question that emerged after the Cold War was whether we still live in this condition. The second problem was connected to a shift in the centre-periphery model that underpins studies of globalization and mobility (see Appadurai, 1990), and to the fact that various 'Others', 'repressed Eastern European cultures and post-colonial societies' (Bradbury, 1995:770), began to speak back in various ways. Soon it

> became clear as the dust of historical transformation settled [that] the triumph of free expression and the elaboration of the heroes and heroines of dissent did not produce a new cultural millennium any more than it did a political one. (Ibid.:772)

Johannes Birringer also summarizes this issue by claiming that the arrival of the postcolonial moment in Europe (by postcolonial implying, I presume, the disintegration of the Soviet Union) did not resolve contradictions of the capitalist/socialist opposition (Birringer 2003:27). If then, as Bradbury and Birringer assert, the end of grand modernist meta-narratives did not liberate subjects of Eastern Europe nor did it create a healthier political climate, how can we still discuss postmodernism today? How are we, then, to approach the analysis of the 'contemporary' in arts, politics, or dance? How are we then to understand these 'Other' voices that speak and other bodies that dance in numerous and sometimes unpredictable ways?

Dance studies can be seen as a 'perfect model' for investigating these kinds of 'confusions'. Tensions that cut across the discipline, most notably those of disparately different approaches to dance analysis, are partly a consequence of the inability of dance scholars to define a 'condition' in which we live, dance, and write about dance. Tensions and disputes in dance scholarship still rotate around terms of modernism and postmodernism understood simultaneously as a 'condition', artistic style and/or methodological approach.

The first tension could be seen to reflect an inability of dance scholars to agree on what modernism and postmodernism is in dance. Sally Banes (1987), in her much acclaimed and widely cited *Terpsichore in Sneakers,* connects postmodernism in dance with the practice and the legacy of a few choreographers and dancers gathered around the Judson Church theatre during the 1960s and 1970s in New York. According to Banes, postmodern choreographers, most notably Yvonne Rainer, 'invented' pedestrian movements and introduced non-dance bodies into dance pieces as a radical demystification of dance. Consequently, postmodern dance can comprise 'nothing but pedestrian movement and tasks such as mattress carrying' (Scott, 1997). Banes identifies postmodern dance practice as one that openly questions the nature of dance through the dancing/choreographic process. She states that for postmodern choreographers 'The problem of defining dance was related to the inquiries into time, space, and the body, but extended beyond them, embracing the other arts and asserting propositions about the nature of dance' (Banes, 1987:xix).

According to Banes, Rainer's manifesto can be seen as one of the paradigmatic examples of the postmodern dance aesthetic:

> NO to spectacle no to virtuosity no to transformations and magic and makebelieve no to glamour and transcendency of the star image no to the heroic and the anti-heroic no to trash imagery no to involvement of performer or spectator no to style no to camp no to seduction of spectator by the wiles of the performer no to eccentricity no to moving or being moved. (Rainer, 1965, cited in Banes, 1987:43)

If anything can be dance, how can we know and write about dance at all, and how can we distinguish it from various forms of performance art (see Scott, 1997)? Banes argues that 'the postmodern choreographers proposed that a dance was a dance not because of its content but because of its context—i.e., simply because it was framed as a dance'

(Banes, 1987:xix). Banes's work was challenged (see Manning, 1988; Scott, 1997; Carlson, 2004) as it was influential, showing profound changes in dance and in the way dance scholarship thought about dance.[7]

The second tension could be seen as a tension between what has come to be seen as modernist and postmodernist approaches to dance analysis. Modernist approaches are seen as those that combine detailed description/formal analysis of a dance piece and historical contextualization. According to Jackson (1994), this kind of approach is exemplified in the early writing of Janet Adshead in which she argues for a so-called 'dance-based dance theory'. Adshead writes that: 'much of what a choreographer does is, of necessity, a product of her or his training, the techniques that that person has studied, the works they have danced in and seen and the conventions and traditions that these derive from' (Adshead, 1987, cited in Jackson, 1994:3). Adshead suggests a formal analysis of a dance score (repetition, variations, motif development) be put in historical, cultural, and biographical contexts and this would then amount to a more or less plausible interpretation of a dance piece (ibid.).

Postmodernist approaches to dance are usually identified as derivates from poststructuralism and deconstruction, where dance came to be seen as a signifying practice that occurs within a system of power relations. For

---

[7] These changes refer to the shift in dance studies that originated from the Judson Church project from considering dance as theatre art, to analyzing dance as performance art. This consequently redefined the methodology of dance studies which then shifted its focus away from movement analysis, towards the question of the essence of performing (see Lepecki, 2004b).

Jackson (1994), an example of this kind of approach to dance is found in the work of Susan Foster. In *Reading Dancing* Foster states: 'Once the body, the subject, and the expressive act have been "denaturalized", then the dance can be examined explicitly as a system of codes and conventions that support its meaning' (Foster, 1986, cited in Jackson, 1994:3).

So for Adshead the main question is what dance means in a certain context, whereas for Foster the main concern is how dance makes meanings in a certain context. With the influence of poststructuralism, dance was granted a more significant role and dance scholarship finally moved from being a marginal discipline and entered into a debate about major concerns developed within philosophy, literature, and arts. As Thomas observed:

> poststructuralism, postmodernism and feminism have instigated their respective attacks on the human subject ... they have revealed the centrality of the body as a site of discourse and social control. They have elucidated how bodies have become objectified and subjectified through a range of discourses [and therefore] have contributed further to the possibility of dance being afforded a more substantial cultural voice. (Thomas, 1995, cited in Carter, 2004b:11)

Ramsay Burt, writing about these influences of social sciences on dance scholarship, claims that the majority of works on dance by the end of the 1990s were concerned with establishing 'a history of canonical artists using methodologies which were largely positivist and informed by liberal, modernist ideologies of aesthetic value' (Burt, 2000:125-6). Often these approaches explored the ways in which ideologies are inscribed in dance, notably by exploring gender representation in classical ballet. However, by the end of the 1990s, according to Burt, the most progressive dance scholarship moved towards what he identifies as a post-identitarian stance, with the emergence of queer, poststructuralist, and postcolonial theories (see also Desmond, 2000).

This change finally introduced the theorization of the body into dance scholarship, even if only insofar as the dance score and the dancer's body were perceived as any other texts of culture. This, however, does not mean that dance scholarship fully embraced these changes. Burt actually identifies a sort of reassessment at work in dance studies which is a consequence of shifts in the humanities as modernist methods slowly started to give way to post-modernist ones. He claims that concern has been expressed that dance studies theorized in a postmodern way might lose sight of actual dancing. Consequently:

> Some dance scholars, worried at the seeming dilution of what they see as the specificity of dance studies through the use of methodologies imported from film theory and cultural studies, are beginning to articulate what could perhaps be described as a call back to the basics of dance scholarship. (Burt, 2000:177)

By 'basics' he means detailed historical contextualization informed by a traditional belief in the aesthetic value of dance as art, which Burt, from his perspective, deplores. Roger Copeland, on the other hand, can be seen as a dance scholar who laments the influence of poststructuralism on dance analysis. When detecting various influences of poststructuralism and deconstruction on dance scholarship he confesses that he speaks as:

> someone fundamentally unsympathetic to the sort of jargonized, overly methodologized 'theories' that have come to dominate academic approaches to the arts over the past fifteen years. Perhaps, it's a blessing in disguise that dance studies—despite the steadily increasing influence of deconstruction, post-structuralism, and gender-politics—remain comparatively 'under-theorized'. (Copeland, 1998:100–1)

These tensions being unresolved, the field of dance studies today appears to be simultaneously 'under-theorized' and 'over-theorized', especially since at the beginning of the 1990s, dance scholarship was challenged not by other disciplines but by dance itself, as a generation of young choreographers started engaging with and creating their work through philosophy.

André Lepecki identifies new tendencies in European dance practice that openly explore dance through philosophy, showing that the supposedly stable relationship between 'dance' and 'choreography' is undermined by certain philosophical concepts. Thus, Lepecki observed, that as contemporary European choreography 'treads the wavering, plundered ground of choreography, one could say that the major mode of operation is that of reduction. A reduction of the expansive, of the spectacular, of the unessential' (Lepecki, 2004b:179). The essential concern of conceptual dance, according to Lepecki, is to reduce choreography in resistance to the spectacular.

However, this resistance 'has to be seen not only as the aesthetic reduction (which would side with minimalist concerns) but importantly as a political statement of the market value of the dance object' (ibid.). Pouillaude also clarifies this difference between the minimalist aesthetic of postmodern movements in dance during the 1960s (identified as postmodern dance by Banes) and current tendencies in European choreography. He terms the changes in European dance a 'mutation' which, 'announces a radical change of the regime within the production of the works' (Pouillaude, 2007:130). Thus he says:

> Whereas postmodern dance was understood as the analytic questioning of an essence (what is dance?), operating by eidetic variation and testing the limits (how far can one go without ceasing to produce dance?) our mutation seems rather to shift the questioning towards the essence of performing (to what extent is there an event when I do something — or not — in front of somebody who does not do anything?) (ibid.:132)

Drawing on the practice of new European dance, sometimes termed Not-dance (Birringer, 2005), Lepecki suggests that there is a certain potentiality when dance entangles with philosophy. In 'Dance Composes Philosophy Composes Dance', a special edition of *The Drama Review* [TDR] dedicated to dance, he states some of the goals and hopes for this new approach to dance (and) philosophy. He specifies:

> When philosophy thinks and experiments with dance, when dance thinks and experiments with philosophy, there is the potential for a certain silly frisson, coming from the titillation of joining the rarified air of philosophy with the sweaty efforts of dance. It is not this effect that is the most productive one for dancers and philosophers. What matters is precisely what kind of 'mutant production of enunciation' of subjectivity such encounters generate. (Lepecki, 2006a:19)

Lepecki's writings, through his dedication to the 'new dance practice' and a particular branch of European philosophy, are highly significant, since he has been engaged in the European dance scene for almost two decades. During this period the 'new dance practice'[8] has had its own development and this dynamic is encapsulated in Lepecki's writings which are oriented towards the particular dance aesthetics and politics of the generation of Western European choreographers who were developing their practices during the 1990s. Furthermore, during this time Europe underwent some profound changes, and some 'other' voices and other bodies have entered the field of European dance production. That is why Lepecki's project is useful when entering a discussion about the relation between dance and 'contemporaneity', or between dance and context.

Empire as a Contemporary 'Condition' of Modernity
The European choreographers[9] of the new generation that figure predominantly in Lepecki's writings on contemporary dance practice and critique, make a powerful statement about subjectivity by dismantling the modernist notion of the body and movement in dance. Bojana Kunst describes this development in dance practice and theory since the 1980s as an 'increasing need for theory and reflection' (Kunst, 2010a:80). Their work developed under the influence of poststructuralist theory and Deleuzian philosophy which underpins new ethical modes of being, new subjects-in-

---

[8] Below, for reasons of clarity, the dance tendencies that Lepecki identifies and writes about will be referred as 'the new dance practice'.
[9] These choreographers are: Xavier Le Roy, Jérôme Bel, Boris Charmatz from France; Thomas Lehmen, Sasha Waltz, Felix Ruckert from Germany; La Ribot from Spain; Vera Mantero from Portugal; and Jonathan Burrows from United Kingdom, to name just a few (see Lepecki, 2004b:171).

becoming bound by sensation, expression and affect which superseded 'self-enclosed' modernist subjects bound by fixed notions of identity. Yet, I would stress, this call for another kind of subjectivity assumes it to be outside, escaping the production and regulation of subjectivities within what Lepecki terms the 'condition' of 'contemporary modernity'. Lepecki associates 'contemporary modernity' with a particular mode of subjectivity. Rather than aligning modernity with the rise of industrial capitalism, which is one of the possible approaches Lepecki considered, he prefers to identify it with the mode of the 'self-sufficient subject: subject that experiences his or her being as fully and ontologically independent from the world' (Lepecki, 2006b:11).

Additionally, he claims, following Homi Bhabha, that the colonial condition is the intrinsic condition of modernity. Therefore, he concludes that 'as long as the colonial condition exists (no matter in what guise) there will be no closure of modernity' (ibid:15). This can be understood as a powerful statement against understandings of post-modernism as a transition to an age without history that can cure all the 'maladies of modernity'. However, there is a problem with Lepecki's usage of the term modernity to encapsulate the contemporary operation of capitalist production. According to Hardt and Negri (2000), today we cannot speak any more of modernism in terms of capitalist production, but we are witnessing the postmodernization of the global economy. If we revisit Lepecki's statement, it is therefore important precisely in what guise the colonial condition exists today. Hardt and Negri call this emergent imperial sovereignty Empire. This new paradigm of imperial sovereignty replaces older modernist models of sovereignty and as such it is not a metaphor, but a concept that is:

characterized fundamentally by a lack of boundaries ... Empire posits a regime that effectively encompasses the spatial totality. [Further,] Empire presents itself as an order that effectively suspends history and thereby fixes the existing state of affairs for eternity ... as a regime with no temporal boundaries and in this sense outside of history and or at the end of history. [And finally,] Empire not only manages a territory and a population but also creates the very world it inhabits. It not only regulates human interactions but also seeks directly to rule over human nature. The object of its rule is social life in its entirety, and thus Empire presents the paradigmatic form of biopower. (ibid.:xiv–xv)

As such, Empire creates a different paradigm of subjectivity. To Hardt and Negri, the contemporary theoretical insistence of fluid subjectivities, and the postcolonial insistence on hybridity set against binary divisions, do not represent a resistance to the ongoing redistribution of power, but are themselves a symptom of the passage from modern to imperial sovereignty.

I suggest that Lepecki's project and the practice of his dancers can be seen in a similar light. We can consider them not as a subversion of dominant modes of subjectivity but as a practice of a certain contemporary mode of subjectivity. The subject-in-becoming, I would argue, is a privilege of certain Western subjects notwithstanding the fact that it aims to dismantle the very boundary between East and West, Self and Other, human and animal.

The very understanding of what the subject is, is perhaps one of the central concepts of the Empire. Hardt and Negri, following Foucault, claim that 'In the post-modernization of the global economy, the creation of wealth production, the production of social life itself' (ibid.:xiii). As

Morris has pointed out, Hardt and Negri also use the idea of human as a desiring machine developed by Deleuze and Guattari to refer to:

> a control that extends into the minds and bodies of its subjects so that the subjects reproduce the power autonomously as part of their own constitutions. This power becomes an integral part of the reproduction of life itself ... the new imperial power is 'absolute' since it is completely immanent to 'the ontological machine of production and reproduction'. (Morris, 2004:128–9)

Marina Gržinić (2009) also follows this Foucaultian understanding of biopolitics as biopower, whose aim is the production and reproduction of life itself. According to her, biopower today includes not only the production and reproduction of subjects but 'the regulation and understanding of what the process of subjectification means in itself' (ibid.). If I understand her correctly, she is suggesting that the whole interest in subjectivity and the process of subjectification in dance and dance scholarship is itself a result, an effect of imperial sovereignty. This does not necessarily mean that dance practices identified by Lepecki and the theoretical writings about dance can simply be discarded as a full manifestation of the new sovereignty. After all, as Bauer points out, it would be simplistic to argue that the 'performing arts are making the case for the wildest form of capitalism' (Bauer, 2008:16). Yet, instead of simply proclaiming some dance practices as having more liberatory potential in subverting modernist modes of subjectification, it is important to situate the political potentiality of dance in the dynamic of the production of the social under contemporary regimes of biopolitics.[10] This is exactly where Hardt and Negri disagree with Deleuze's and Guattari's understanding of desire. Although they use the idea of desire as both a productive and reproductive force within the political, they reject the notion that desire is rhizomatic in nature. Thus they state that: 'Deleuze and Guattari discovered the productivity of social production (creative production, production of values, social relations, affects and becomings), but managed to articulate it only superficially and ephemerally, as a chaotic, indeterminate horizon marked by the ungraspable event' (Hardt and Negri, 2000:28).

Hardt and Negri, in contrast, situate this dynamic of social production and its relation to biopower in the new nature of productive labour, which they call 'immaterial labor' (ibid.:28-9). Dance may well provide a privileged analytical window here, since 'the independent artist is most often identified as the paradigmatic example of immaterial labour' (Bauer, 2008:16) or as Pang (2009) identified as an example of a creative worker in the expanding creative industries.

The dancers that I have been working with can all be called immaterial workers, working in creative industries, deploying concepts and ideas, and creating immediate and affective relations within global dance communities. Most of them value process-oriented work which, although usually discussed under the frame of the new aesthetic paradigm of contemporary dance, is increasingly recognized to be

---

[10] Thomas identifies this tendency in dance studies especially in connection to postmodern dance where the 'idea of a "postmodernism of resistance" [serves] as a yardstick by which to measure other dance practices' (Thomas, 1996:75).

connected to 'the wider economic and cultural contexts of work processes, with immaterial labour in general' (Kunst, 2010a:83). We have already seen that the fact that dance does not produce material objects (although it works most immediately with the materiality of the body), i.e. its ephemeral nature, has been privileged as its exclusive potential of resistance. Moreover, in Hardt and Negri's writing, the revolutionary and resisting potential within Empire lies in the affective labour of precisely immaterial workers. These two equations put together would mean that dancers and dancing activity is a doubly privileged site for resistance and that, however we interpret it, dance is always about resistance. This book however will not write about dance practices as resistant or at least not as necessarily resistant. What interests me more is cautious questioning and tracing ideas and bodies as they travel across borders, powerful and affective networking under the watchful and restrictive gaze of Empire. This resonates with Gille and Ó Riain's understanding that we should see 'globalization as a repatterning of fluidities and mobilities on the one hand and stoppages and fixities on the other, rather than an all-encompassing world of fluidity' (Gille and Ó Riain 2002:275).

The strongest theoretical and methodological argument that marks recent writings on labour, launched either from the corner of the discussions on globalization and/or of the new regime of labour, is precisely the fact of the increased mobility of bodies, concepts, and ideas across the globe, and related to this phenomenon, the emergent question of the meaning of space and otherness in a globalized world.

4. Globalization, Hybridity, and Contemporary Dance

Mobility became one of the major tropes in discussions about globalization. In this sense, globalization mainly refers to phenomena such as migration, borderlands, transnational social movements, cross-border networks, diasporas, new electronic media, and the emergence of 'global civil society' (Eley, 2007) in the context of worldwide expansion of free market politics. Although discussions on globalization often include questioning whether the phenomenon is indeed novel (Gikandi, 2000), there is an implicit consensus that there is a new quality of mobility which includes all interconnected phenomena mentioned above. Sadowski-Smith (1999), claims that the academic contributions on globalization often follow Immanuel Wallerstein's thesis of the world-system as a global capitalist economy and/or restrict their inquiries to the last decade of the twentieth century. For instance, to Fredric Jameson (1991) and David Harvey (1989), globalization mainly refers to the movement of advanced industrial societies from standardized mass production to diverse flexible production, and creates a grim picture of a culture that stresses superficiality and ignores historical contextualizations. At the other end of the spectrum are theoreticians such as Homi Bhabha, who celebrate globalization as an 'empowering condition of hybridity'. Bhabha rejects what he sees as 'the teleological spaces of global capital' with the epistemic and discursive limits of class (Bhabha, 1994:227). This book will identify globalization as a contemporary condition of modernity or Empire in Hardt and Negri's terminology discussed above. This effectively means that although acknowledging positive aspects of globalization, characterized by growth of cultural exchange, it will tirelessly emphasize 'that these cultural transactions [are] characterised by and depend upon existing economic inequalities between metropolitan centers and the peripheries' (Chowdhury, 2006:130).

The dance world can be seen as a privileged analytical tool for examining both globalization as a current restructuring of power relations and mobility, in the sense of both quite literally moving bodies across borders and places, and more generally dance as a 'reflexive mobilization of the body … a social process that foregrounds the very means through which bodies gather' (Martin, 1998:6). In the introduction to the 2008 issue of the *Dance Research Journal* dedicated to the philosophical and analytical links between dance and migration studies, editor Paul Scolieri notes that dance and migration share common ground because the dance world is a nomadic one constituted by a mobile set of subjects in search of economic prosperity and/or political and artistic freedoms. Despite the fact that Scolieri's words certainly have a ring of truth, dance scholarship rarely addresses these links and emphasizes more liberatory aspects of dance nomadism exemplified by exciting and ground breaking examples of artistic collaboration across borders. Here I shall contest these often implied narratives of globalization as 'free flows across borders', in which moving away from home and migration are set as ways of thinking, because they serve to 'erase the real and substantive differences between the conditions in which particular moves across spatial borders take place' (Ahmed, 2000:80, see also Di Stefano, 2002). We shall see that no matter how dancers construct and understand what and where their home is, it always depends on the (im)possibility of leaving it, of crossing borders that are both symbolic and real. Narratives related by my dancers tirelessly emphasize the importance of real existing borders and geopolitical locations that have an immense effect on their careers and professional lives.

Moreover, it will become clear that even touching questions such as that of dance aesthetics is geopolitically grounded—since 'aesthetic principles, values and vocabularies organize where art works and produces meaning in time and space' (Hamera, 2007:3). The space that this book addresses is the space of Eastern Europe in the time after the collapse of the Cold War divisions, i.e. in the time when Eastern Europe found itself emerging from a '"post-historical" experiment in supranationalism to the "historical" horizon of politics based on such social tangibles as common language, religion, memories and a "traditional relation to place"'(Resina, 2003:46). Three out of the four dancers that figure in this research are from Eastern Europe, one of them from the former Soviet Bloc, and their careers have been evolving in a time of profound shifts and redefinitions of identities in the process of European integration in what Etienne Balibar calls the crisis connected to 'the meaning we attach to the name "Europe"'(Balibar, 2003:36). Balibar further claims that the bloody wars that followed the disintegration of the former Yugoslavia intensified this question giving it a particularly dramatic form. Indeed the Balkan wars created a common ground on which European intellectuals and politicians could take stances and air views on the issues relating to the integration of their own societies and problematic histories (von Oppen, 2006). For instance, Julia Kristeva, a much acclaimed French theorist of Bulgarian origin, in the text 'Bulgaria, My Suffering' (2000) glorifies French civilization embedded in the notion of civil society, and rejects her native country. Bulgaria to her, along with other Balkan countries, represents, 'tribal nationalism and the new civic threat to civil society' (Kristeva, 2000, cited in Bjelić, 2006:37). She argues that this is exemplified in the chaotic and dirty streets of Sofia, the Bulgarian capital, and in dirty Bulgarian language, that, quite literally, cannot speak the 'enlightened' language of civil Europe. I will not devote space here to address the issues of representation and power relations to critique Kristeva in depth. This critique is already existing and quite elaborate within the field of the so-called Balkan studies inaugurated by Maria Todorova's seminal study *Imagining the Balkans* (1997). Dušan Bjelić (2006) analyzed in some detail Kristeva's text as well. Instead I wish to address the institutional, cultural, and life changes that resulted after the fall of socialism and the historical trajectory of Western capitalism will be the backdrop of these debates. In many ways I could follow Vicky Unruh's writing on postsocialist Cuba to illuminate the sort of conditions and changes that the fall of socialism in South East Europe instigated:

> Cuba, although embracing selective capitalist elements to fend off economic disaster, could be characterized as the embodiment of late twentieth-century *socialism under siege*. But its singularities notwithstanding, the Cuban case foregrounds the power of a sudden financial crisis to catapult the secure into precariousness and shake up a society's dearly held guiding myths about value of work and the equality of access for citizens. (Unruh, 2012:733, my emphasis)

I wish to pause here. Although this book will not engage in an in-depth study of postsocialist countries as such, I find Unruh's phrase 'socialism under siege' extremely potent in understanding the backdrop of many stories and narratives in this study. Moreover, with the dancers I interviewed the economic crisis of 2008 that devastated so many, was an important moment of transition to precariousness—dancers felt that their right to work and make a living was under siege. As my study progressed the effect of helplessness and vulnerability was increasingly 'in the air'. However, this study also questions the issue of representation coupled by the issues of power and redistribution. The following section will address the interrelationships of identity, marginality, and hybridity as developed within postcolonial and poststructuralist scholarship. These tropes will be examined through the lenses of postsocialist studies.

Understanding Postsocialism: Identity and Hybridity
In the poststructuralist discussions surrounding the intersections of art, politics, and literature the critical resistance position was given to the marginalized identities and voices that were often unrepresented in Western hegemonic discourse. Thus, hybrid identities, 'border identities' that transgress or blur the border between self and the 'Other', were deemed subversive as they disrupt the binary logic of Western modernist thought. For instance, Kompridis argues that:

> Although [hybridity] is a concept neither uniformly understood nor uniformly applied ... it is predominantly deployed as a boundary-subverting, unquestionably transgressive, critical tool [and it] has undergone a premature, largely unnoticed normativization, thereby making available a framework within which the political claims of culture can be tamed and domesticated. (Kompridis, 2005:320-2)

Homi Bhabha is perhaps the most influential postcolonial scholar to launch the idea of cultural hybridity and hybrid identities. A hybrid identity is an impure, syncretic identity,

What is Dance?

as it does not imply a safe encounter that consolidates differences or releases tension between cultures but it is 'the split screen of the self and its doubling' (Bhabha, 1994:113-14; also in Marciniak, 2009). In discussing the precise meaning of this term in Bhabha's work Sanjoy Roy clarifies:

> We all, in fact, have plural identities that shift with context, place and time, often in contradictory ways; in short, we are all hybrids. But this ordinary, everyday hybridity is not generally conceived as such: hybridity seems to be recognized only when its elements are seen as somehow essentially incompatible; that is when a cultural line has been crossed, such as the imaginary one between East and West. (Roy, 1997:83)

This quotation emphasizes precisely two interrelated problems of the concept as often employed by scholars and critics. First as mentioned above, East and West alike are essentialized as 'essentially incompatible' and this condition appears as being outside historical circumstances and contexts (Ahmad, 2008). The second, interrelated problem is the emphasis on an imaginary line between East and West. What exactly is meant here by 'imaginary'? Are we claiming that this line is imaginary because it does not really exist any longer in the globalized world? Or does imaginary refer to discourses around existing national borders? Too often, this difference is not specified and the 'border' that works as a metaphor in academic writing is not a physical or even mental demarcation line between different 'nation-states', but it has come to be seen as a metaphor for liminal subjectivities that live across and negotiate multiple ethnic, racial, linguistic, and sexual lines (Fox, 1994). As Claire Fox specifies: 'when the border is spatialized in these theories, that space is almost always universal. The Third World having been collapsed into the First' (ibid.:61).

Similarly, Arif Dirlik (1998) in his *Postcolonial Aura* argues that postcolonial theorists tend to assume that 'representations of the world in fiction suffice as evidence, that the production and negotiation of meaning in literary encounters is all that matters' (Palat, 2000; see also Cook and Harrison, 2003) and this work of postcolonial scholars goes against the grain of historical scholarship based on empirical evidence. From a somewhat different standpoint, but pointing to similar problems, Sara Ahmed (1999, 2000) criticizes the contemporary discourses of multiculturalism, arguing that the contemporary Western subject is constantly called to unmake the 'border' between self and the racially marked 'Other', to move along the hybrid self-Other border, and consume and incorporate the 'Other'. The 'stranger', the 'Other', according to her, thus becomes a fetish, that is, 'the figure of stranger with a life of its own insofar as [it is cut off from] the histories of its determination' (Ahmed: 2000:5).

Among the Eastern European postsocialist scholars there have been some efforts to employ the concept of hybridity to address Eastern European/postsocialist 'difference'. Katarzyna Marciniak proposes the concept of 'postsocialist hybridity' to capture 'contradictions, ambivalences and startling contrasts which have emerged in the post Berlin-Wall period' (Marciniak, 2009:175). Contradictions and ambivalences related to Eastern European 'difference' are especially visible in the field of gender studies and the concept of hybridity did not seem to be able to offer any conceptual or methodological solutions. Thus, feminist work, relying on a dialogue between Western and postsocialist feminists, explores the challenge of trying to identify and theorize gender issues important to post–state socialist societies, in the shadow of an already well-established feminist legacy from North America and Western Europe (Cerwonka, 2008:811; Ousmanova, 2003). These dialogues often emphasize the inadequacy of applying concepts developed in Western feminism to postsocialist societies and the concept of difference is often employed as an 'imperfect solution to Western hegemony' (Cerwonka, 2008:816). Thus to Cerwonka, conceptual inadequacies of the liberal pluralist model of difference, reproduce rather than eliminate, uneven power relations in global feminism. Apart from the conceptual inadequacies relating to the East-West dialogue in feminism, there seems to be an even greater lack of theorizing about gender relations and masculinities in postsocialist Eastern Europe. Pat Simpson, in *Peripheralizing Patriarchy* (2004), claims that in reality body-based artwork has been a major means of representing the identity crisis related to masculinities in Central and Eastern Europe rather than academic engagement. In her view, the alleged theme of these art works is the so-called 'collapse of patriarchy' by which some practices seem to represent economic and social marginality and could be seen as a loss of national and personal identity. On the other hand, there are also practices that point to the survival and intensification of patriarchy, phallocentrism, and sexism.

My choice to work with male dancers for this book thus addresses these interrelated issues of the simultaneous empowerment and marginality of male dancers within the theatrical dance world and within the social and political spaces they inhabit Although none of them has an explicit body art/dance practice in the way Simpson is indicating, their narratives relating to 'becoming a dancer' in Turkey and Eastern Europe saliently reveal much about gender relations and dynamics in these societies. In short, since many problems relating to the theorizing of gender and masculinity in postsocialist countries spring from the inability of scholars to take issue with the theorizing of gender relations during socialism, stories about growing up during socialism, at least in some of those narratives, might serve as an appropriate window for thinking about gender relations in Eastern Europe.

To what extent the reader will find these narratives 'different' from his/her own experiences is open to interpretation. Feminist scholars from Eastern Europe often try to argue that regardless of the fact that political leaders from both sides of the Iron Curtain emphasized difference and inferiority of life on the 'other side', borders were never hermetically sealed and the complexity of ideas and influences travelled across the borders well before globalization (Olsen, 1997). Olsen concludes that 'To the extent that Westerners view Central and Eastern Europeans as Other, it is argued, they will never understand the region or be able to help its people' (ibid.:2222).

The ideas related to 'otherness' and 'difference' also seem to be affecting the dance world and appear to be a symptom of 'Dance under globalization' (Savigliano, 2009:169). Martha Savigliano identifies World Dance as a powerful rubric of dance under globalization that employs a plethora of scholars, critics, and producers that select and shape the kind of dancing and dancers that constitute World Dance. She adds that 'All dancing (that "thing" that dancers do) obviously takes place in the world, but not all of it amounts to World Dance' (ibid.:165). Savigliano's words resonate with Bourdieu's (1993) idea of fields of cultural production. In his 'The Field of Cultural Production, or: The Economic World Reversed' Bourdieu (1993) describes art fields as social worlds with their own power dynamic, yet subordinated to larger power structures in society. It is precisely the internal dynamic within the field and between fields themselves that constitute and shape legitimate art practices and a particular art aesthetic. Savigliano, for instance, proclaims that the field of World Dance favours 'particular kinds of dances that work at fascinating with difference as they elicit culturally progressive cosmopolitan values' (Savigliano, 2009:165).

Similarly to Savigliano, albeit from different angle, Judith Hamera claims that 'aesthetics are inherently social' (2007). Hamera develops a methodological approach she calls the social work of aesthetics by which she assumes that:

> The formal properties and presumptions intrinsic to the production and consumption of art are communicative currency developed by and circulating between artists, audiences and critics, binding them together in interpretive communities, serving as bases for exchange in the public and private conversations that constitute art's relational, political and affective lives. (Hamera, 2007:3)

Hamera further explicates that the understanding of the social work of aesthetic is especially central to performance since its creative process is explicitly communal and corporeal. The issue is taken further by Shannon Jackson who states, when questioning the notion of artistic autonomy, that:

> Questions of aesthetic autonomy gain an acute urgency when we consider what it means to sustain not only the life of art but also the lives of artists. In fact, the variation in content, form, and goal in social practice and experimental art subtly interacts with artists' differing sense of where they will find security of employment. (Jackson, 2011:16)

The importance of Jackson's assertion is not only the way she seeks to illuminate the interdependence of the aesthetics and systems of funding, but the way she connects these questions to the deeper meaning of sustainability of artists' lives. This issue will be perhaps the core of this book. By this I mean not only the questioning of gender transgressions when men take professional roles traditionally occupied by women. Neither the detailed questioning of work and mobility patterns quite exhausts the topic. The issue of sustainability is perhaps taken on the basic level of methodology through my refusal to deal with performance events but, instead, to devote my study to questioning of dance environments (Berlant, 2007) or atmospheres (Brennan, 2004) — or what I call 'backstage economies'. What I try to capture by this term is perhaps already beautifully captured by Lyotard's musings on events and everyday occurrences:

> There are many events whose occurrence doesn't offer any matter to be confronted, many happenings inside of which nothingness remain hidden and imperceptible, events without barricades. They come to us concealed under the appearance of everyday occurrences. To become sensitive to their quality as actual events ... requires at the very least a high degree of refinement in the perception of small differences. (Lyotard, 1988:18)

The attention to small and substantial differences either of gender, nationality, or class is the core task of this study which I trace through everyday occurrences or 'backstage economies'. These backstage economies will be addressed in Chapter Two through my questioning of changing cultural policies in multicultural Europe and changing dance scenes in South East Europe. This chapter will introduce my research material giving it some sound methodological and theoretical grounding. Chapter Three will address the question of masculinity in contemporary dance through my South East European material. The exploration of gender in Western theatrical dance is perhaps one of the most debated and explored topics in dance studies. These debates on gender were mainly conveyed through the questioning of female agency in ballet rendering the question of masculinity in theatrical dance somewhat neglected. My take on the question of gender in dance is, therefore, through an almost exclusive focus on masculinity in dance explored through the mainly childhood narratives of my dancers, that also offers a picture of growing up under the turbulent and difficult socialist and postsocialist times. This chapter will also involve further discussion on gender and (post) socialism addressing the aforementioned feminist dialogues across the East/West divide. Following these debates on postsocialism, Chapter Four will expand the topic by questioning the issue of labour in dance by addressing the working and living patterns of dancers as creative workers under the contemporary cognitive capitalism. Further, this chapter will most emphatically address the question of globalization and the new regime of labour, especially under the backdrop of impending economic crisis. In this chapter dancers openly discuss dance technique and the tension between dance as body labour, and dance as a creative research. This discussion of labour, then, returns to the more theoretical question of dance as produced by human bodies working to a given technique and creating affective communities, however fragile those may be, across the globe.

Chapter Five will take a glance on precisely this presumed power of dance to create and recreate communities anew. It will address the mobility and community building patterns of the dancers in question. The final remarks in Chapter Five will also give some further comments on dance methodology by following Foster's (1996a) proposition that, rather than approaching dance through already established methodologies developed within other disciplines, we should question the methodologies and theoretical perspectives through dance. This call is not, however, exclusively methodological but it is also crucial in addressing recent philosophical writings on dance that emphasize its affective and political potential connected to its embodied nature (Puchner, 2002). From the general question of the nature and ethic of dance performance, the final and concluding remarks will turn to the ethic of dance and its affective and community sustaining potential.

CHAPTER 2

SHATTERED AND SOWN EUROPE: THEORETICAL QUESTIONS AND METHODOLOGICAL APPROACHES TO STUDY DANCE UNDER GLOBALIZATION

1. End of the Cold War and Cultural Policies in Europe

> And my life? Apart from constantly changing realities and contexts like a tout in front of the cinema ..., and by constantly travelling to and fro, I'm realizing how cultural institutions endeavour on developing local artistic communities and the survival of local artists. You can see this in Germany. For example this year, out of all young and aspiring choreographers, funding for projects for the next year is allocated exclusively to Germans (i.e. German citizens) and also those who are already somehow supported institutionally or academically, that is, those already part of the system. Or for instance in Sweden — MDT theatre supports young Swedish artists that came from schools like MA DOCH, PARTS, and SNDO ... and by that builds local community, but also internationally works on the image of Sweden as not any longer on the periphery of the artistic world. In Amsterdam, the theatre that is led by Bojana Mladenović now really supports local artists, who have international reputation, but they always have somewhere to return.
>
> In this sense, I'm realizing, since I'm neither German, nor Swedish, nor Dutch, I don't have any chance of being supported institutionally. (Koruga, 2013)

Cultural institutions across Europe are directly implicated in both labour policies fostered by the European Union (EU) and in crafting 'a new kind of European cultural imagination' which became a priority after the Cold War

(Meinhof and Triandafyllidou, 2006:3). The fall of the Berlin Wall and the incorporation of the so-called Second World into the circulation of world capitalism, represent not only huge visible changes on the European map, but also global political, economic, and ideological shifts. The violent and peaceful dissolutions of many Eastern European countries have motivated Mexican American artist Guillermo Gómez-Peña to use Eastern Europe as a metaphor for the hybridization and fragmentation of America in his performance The New World Border. The hybridization of language and the spectacle of micro republics just 'popping up everywhere' were to 'force the [American] audience to experience the cultural vertigo of living in a multilingual/multiracial society' (Gómez-Peña, 1996:21). The above statement of the dancer Igor Koruga testifies partly to that vertigo, the constant shifting ground of the new European identities, where travelling artists may hold a privileged position in their performative manifestations. However, something else is significant here: this statement was made in 2013, almost twenty-four years after the fall of the Berlin Wall, and it seems that another, more salient wall has been put in place. I refer here to the process of solidification and militarization of the EU borders in what Matthew Carr re-termed 'Fortress Europe' (Carr, 2012). Although the term refers to the treatment of refugees trying to reach Europe from faraway places, it is equally significant for countries bordering the EU, as its 'immediate outside' (Jansen, 2009). My research focuses precisely on these countries which are close but not close enough, whose citizens may enter the Union but cannot stay, and who can spend the money as tourists but cannot, as Igor testifies, earn money through work. But more will be said about work.

    The fall of socialism in Eastern Europe and the disappearance of the so-called Second World posed a significant challenge to both Western and Eastern European scholarship. Although logically this would also result in the disappearance of the Three Worlds model, what happened is that the Second World disappeared from the geographical (and, on the whole, from the academic) maps where First and Third Worlds still figure as entities in remapping the new phase of the capitalist system. This time the First World stands for white, industrialized, Christian, and rich, and the Third World is thought of as non-white, non-industrialized, non-Christian, poor (Ahmad, 2008:310). We also hear about a North-South axis with regard to the circulation of capital, but the First/Third World dichotomy is still very much used. In this conception, the Second World silently became part of the First and has nothing to offer to First and to Third World scholarships.

Many 'Second World', Eastern European scholars argue for the necessity of dialogue among scholars traditionally assigned to deal with the First, Second, or Third Worlds. In the introductory note to a collection of essays on Eastern Europe, Sibelan Forrester, Magdalena J. Zaborovska and Elena Gapova call on Eastern European scholars to introduce interdisciplinary approaches deploying concepts of cultural studies, African American Studies, and postcolonial studies. This, they argue, would enrich Eastern European studies that could also benefit from this interdisciplinary dialogue because 'the exercise of applying theory to a new case offers a useful corrective to a theory, which so far may have focused exclusively on the "global" binary of the First versus Third World' (Forrester, Zaborovska, and Gapova, 2004:4). This is important to know since, according to them, the books that recently appeared on the Second World are almost exclusively on the economy, politics, and sociology, ignoring even the recent past (ibid.).

Jacqui True in *Gender, Globalization and Postsocialism: The Czech Republic After Communism* (2003) similarly claims that the studies of postsocialism, despite their many merits, did not as yet pay much attention to everyday life after communism. The focus has been, as clear from above, on the political, institutional, and economic transformation. We know little, True claims, about the changes in the texture of life of ordinary people. This is exactly what my research aims to capture. Dancers' narratives are important as they reveal both imaginary and literary moves of bodies and ideas across symbolic and real borders: in this case we are discussing the border between the EU and its 'immediate outside'. Further, this strategy puts anthropology and dance studies in close collaboration. On one hand, it provides dance studies with the insight into the social and economic origins of dance aesthetic and practices provided by the methodological advantages of anthropology. On the other hand, the affective faculties of dancing bodies, dance as praxis, and dance networking under globalization might offer to anthropology a fresh approach to the understanding of the practices of 'everyday' in globalization.

In writing on belly dancers and gentrification in Istanbul, Öykü Potuoğlu-Cook reformulated Erving Goffman's dramaturgical metaphor to draw a distinction between 'frontstage' and 'backstage' in studying belly dance in order to historicize the motivations of dancers and other social actors in engaging in dance (Potuoğlu-Cook, 2006). To Potuoğlu-Cook:

> the backstage analysis encompasses pre- and post-performance acts and the fluid yet conflicting presence of other social actors. ... A fluid frontstage and backstage divide implicates not a power-neutral architectural, spatial,

or performative separation ... but, rather, a division of labor and an ongoing power negotiation inflected by class, gender, and religion. (ibid.:646)

Rather than merely studying dance performance aesthetics and politics ('frontstage'), the 'backstage', or rather the 'frontstage' and 'backstage' divide (ibid), is my primary interest in approaching dance in this research.

To return to Jacqui True's call from the beginning, there is one more important caveat to introduce. True claims that transition in Central and Eastern Europe has also involved a significant transformation of gender identities, that is, it involved new forms of feminine and masculine identities shaped by global forces and mediated by local contexts—therefore, True simply tries to 'demonstrate the inextricability of gender and global transformations' (True, 2003:2). To Radel (2001), the sexuality itself is an important epistemological tool in understanding the crisis of representation generated by the fall of communism. Certainly, we could say that postsocialist countries underwent changes in gender identities, the process which sometimes, like in the case of Serbia, is being described as 're-traditionalization' (Golubović, 2006) or as 'demoralisation of men at the lower end of the labour market' as the research in Russia testifies (Ashwin and Lytkina, 2004). However the question of masculine identification in postsocialism is even more challenging as the postsocialist Europe underwent 'the loss of patriarchal narrative and the intensification of patriarchal behaviour' (Simpson, 2004). To question these changes through the case of contemporary dance is even more challenging. Not only because the debates on gender and sexuality are intrinsic to dance studies as 'sexuality and dance share the same instrument—the human body' (Hanna,

1988:xiii);[11] but because the discussion on masculinities is more often to be found in sociology of sport than in either dance or postsocialist studies. My study departed from these several blind spots.

The second important aspect of my research is the slightly overlooked role of 'culture' in rebuilding states in post-socialist societies. By culture here I refer to cultural policies assumed as 'artistic activities and products [that] provide a "natural" linkage between people's everyday lives and broader pattern of political and economic development' (Cash, 2007:1406). The development of cultural policies in the EU clearly came to the fore during the 1990s when there was a sense that a new kind of cultural imagination was needed to foster the project of European unification (Meinhof and Triandafyllidou, 2006:3). A decade later, at the beginning of the new millennium, an increasing number of policy documents were exploring issues around culture, which organized their goals around the development of diversity and democracy (Kiwan and Meinhof, 2006). However, the academic, scholarly output concerning the development of cultural policies in Europe and its 'immediate outside' (Jansen, 2009) and their impact on democratization of postsocialist countries is surprisingly scarce (Murray and Gollmitzer, 2012:564). Jennifer Cash is among the few scholars who addressed this issue in the case of Moldova. She explores the way artists in Moldova negotiate their role in crafting cultural policies in a situation where they are required to work on building new democratic societies whereas, paradoxically, 'these same individuals define their

---

[11] Only one of my dancers is homosexual but his sexual orientation never came forward as important for his professional dance/performance practice.

own professional activities as anti-political and anti-economic' (Cash, 2007:1405).

My own research, although focusing at the outset on the system(s) of funding of arts and cultural policies around contemporary dance in South East Europe, brought me also at the deeper level of engagement, where the policy-based questions opened up deeper and more profound questions of artistic labour. Or, to reiterate, to think about artistic work in this day and age is not only connected with a question of labour policies, but is directly implicated in the larger issues of contemporary global economy. As Schneider and Ridout state 'creativity' mostly associated with artistic work 'also synonymous with neoliberal "innovation," has become oddly twinned with a circulating, affective reliance on terror and threat—the "risks" in artistic and critical innovation [are] strangely linked to increasing economic and environmental unrest' (Ridout and Schneider, 2012:8).

However, before discussing artistic labour in general, several issues around the question of cultural policies should be addressed. As mentioned above, the most potent question around cultural policies in Europe is the question of diversity and multiculturalism connected with migration and integration. There is a rich body of work addressing the historical development of cultural policies around 'migrant cultures' in Europe, such as, for example, a comparative work of Kiwan and Kosnick (2006) on France and Germany. The debates are forged around the existing division between 'high' and 'ethnic' culture in the societies that allow migrant culture to flourish (and provide funding for that) but only under the banner of 'ethnic' culture which usually does not include 'real artistic' merits (ibid.). Although my fieldwork did not include predominantly migrant societies in Western Europe (only one of my dancers does have immigrant status), the dancers, managers, and cultural workers from South East Europe were often discussing their predicaments as artists from Europe's 'immediate outside' at least to a degree by drawing on some sort of migratory experience on different levels. For instance, the Serbian dancer, 'Ivan', when introducing the local dance scene, describes the innate ability of local artists to succeed in the 'big world' precisely because they had to adapt themselves to much harsher life and work conditions:

> I don't know what to say about this ... I simply feel that people here carry a certain code, which may also exist in some other 'difficult' territories in that they went through some very tough times and that they are more capable to cope in different environments. For example, educated people who leave to live abroad really make good life for themselves. For example, I have friends who were barely surviving here, but abroad made a good life because they are used to fighting ... What does it have to do with dance? I don't know ... Simply when people ... some things haven't been discovered yet here. All those stories which have been performed in the West are new here and people are discovering them afresh. All that dealing with acute popular problems, people who are doing them here are starting from the zero, so to speak and they can still genuinely discover certain things. In the West, it's business, art is business, and here there is still that romantic image of the art, but I don't know for how long. I mean, I've already heard that some dancers refuse to perform without being paid and that's it! ('Ivan', 2009)

Although the narrative of the 'succeeding migrant' is not novel and not specific to South East Europe, the quote was worth citing at length because 'Ivan', unwittingly, also explains the specificity of the local scene not in terms of ethnic differences of its actors, but in terms of challenging social conditions, most notably economic hardships. But a similar narrative invoking a 'desire to succeed' is present in further explaining the local dance scene in Serbia and Turkey. Both Serbian dancer 'Maria' and Turkish dancer 'Samir', who were pioneers in building and developing contemporary dance infrastructure in their respective home countries, comment how the recent generations of dancers, just coming out of school, are not used to fighting and creating 'out of nothing', but expect everything to be served for them on the plate—jobs, projects, and careers. In these interviews, the local dance scene in both Serbia and Turkey were rarely discussed in terms of local specificities. Usually they were discussed in comparison with, or in terms of Western European scenes. This is because most of the dancers I interviewed built their careers somewhere between East and West and also because local cultural policies were directly influenced by or tried to comply with EU policies. To invoke Igor's conversation from the beginning, to trace changes in EU policies it is more than sufficient to look at the situation in the work and life of artists who are coming from the countries that are not part of the EU but certainly aspire to be. In Igor's remarks above it is possible to note how he carefully observes and responds to European cultural policies and especially recent 'closing doors' initiatives— funding policies that turn more to artistic communities with the 'right' citizenship but which nevertheless celebrate the 'international' outlook of their scenes. However, as already mentioned, South East European countries have their own dynamic relationship with EU cultural policies, not without optimism but not without many underlying problems as well:

> Eastern and Western Europe cannot easily be subsumed under the same unifying umbrella. Given the inequality that underpins the East-West relationship, Eastern Europeans are involved in a kind of 'knowledge-transfer' exercise. Artistic and cultural agencies are expected—in very different conditions from those obtaining in Western Europe—to promote market driven cultural industries strategies; and they are required, also, to promote political and regional objectives, such as conflict resolution and the combat of stereotypes. In such circumstances, the cultural scene in Eastern Europe finds its development considerably hampered and also distorted. (Meinhof and Triandafyllidou, 2006:16–17)

Meinhof and Triandafyllidou note that this situation leads to the plethora of ambivalent feelings towards Western Europe. There is careful optimism by those countries that could benefit from enlargement process, but also constant fear or marginalization and exclusion from those countries that are left behind. Since 2006, when a study was conducted by Dragićević Šešić and Dragojević, the gap between several South East European countries widened even more with Romania, Bulgaria, and recently Croatia, joining the EU, while Serbia and Macedonia sink deeper into recession and marginalization. Turkey, although miraculously recovering from the recession, is still put aside. And what about contemporary dance in South East Europe? Even within broader discussion on cultural policies, dance has a certain special position (Murray and Gollmitzer, 2012), but dance in South East Europe is a particularly interesting case because it cannot be understood without accounting for EU cultural policies, or more generally, the political and cultural influence of the EU to its 'immediate outside'.

2. Contemporary Dance in South East Europe

To begin with, tracing the history of dance in non-Western spaces is a peculiar endeavour. Ananya Chatterjea (2009), in analyzing traditional Indian Odissi dance, claims that dance historiography from non-Western spaces is always constructed through the Western model that emphasizes modernity with its guiding organizing principles. These historical narratives always mask the strategies of power behind the facade of historical 'facts'. The fact is however that in some cases there is nothing but these versions of history, no 'truth' that needs to be uncovered behind the workings of the power. In former Yugoslavia, for instance, it is only this kind of history of dance we could account for — the historical interrelations of Western and of Yugoslav modernity and, consequently, the history of failure to establish distinct Yugoslav modern dance (Cvejić, 2002). There is no Yugoslav modern dance that would enter the canon of Western dance history. What needs to be addressed in the name of this 'absent' dance history is past and present relations between different versions of modernity. These relations are relations of power in which Western art plays an important material and symbolic role in defining local art practices.

Writing about contemporary dance in Serbia, Ana Vujanović notes the considerable influence of the Soros Foundation on the Serbian dance scene. Contemporary Western dance, she argues, was 'introduced' into the Serbian context during the 1990s and regarded as a Western, democratic practice in opposition to the local regime. Thus, Vujanović observes that:

> Theatrical framing of local dance can also help us to understand the notable interest of SOROS: Fund for an Open Society to support many of these works. In the 1990s it functioned as the main supporter of independent/non-institutional cultural-artistic projects and scenes in the Federal Republic of Yugoslavia, due to its 'advanced' political content, i.e. concretely in the case of Serbia, due to its resistance to Slobodan Milošević's regime. (Vujanović, 2007)

Vujanović thus emphasizes the influence that the structural dependence of the local contemporary dance scene from international funding bodies had on dance aesthetics. The situation, I believe, quite safely can be transferred onto other South East European countries as well. Dragana Alfirević, a dancer from Serbia, also addresses the deep structural and aesthetic impact that contemporary dance developed in Western Europe had on local, Eastern European dance practices:

> Regional dance cannot be observed without taking references from Western Europe, where most of the dancers/choreographers were educated and where they received the information and knowledge about the basis of dance. These bases were so strong throughout the history of regional dance [that] it is now a difficult task to think of it as a purely autonomous form. (Alfirević, cited in Tanurovska, 2007:44)

In line with this, Vujanović argues that there is no local dance history in Serbia and that, therefore, what is considered and practised as contemporary dance in Serbia is contemporary Western dance. In fact, she continues, there is a local dance history but it does not resemble that of Western dance history. There are various 'bodily movement practices' which differ from dance history in Western Europe and the USA. These 'bodily movements' were developed during communism as a means for 'practising' collectivism—we are talking about classical ballet, folklore, and popular dance. Contemporary dance, as such, emerged with foreign support in Serbia during the 1990s and in that sense we can only talk about 'contemporary' dance as Western dance practice. Refining her critical focus on the contemporary dance scene in Serbia, Vujanović cites the Slovenian choreographer Emil Hrvatin who states that contemporary dance cannot exist in non-democratic societies. Vujanović, however, argues that the relevant difference is not one between democratic and non-democratic societies but between socialist and capitalist ones. The '"emancipation of individual" (assigned to democratic societies) is not an opposition of ideology (assigned to non-democratic societies), but is its particular principle' (Vujanović, 2007). Ideologically speaking, she argues, socialist societies prefer 'collectivism' and deny individual bodies and creativity, while capitalist ones, along with the principle of private ownership, prefer 'individualism', self-expressivity, creativity and authorship. Therefore, she states, dance is precisely 'a technological tool for shaping the individual body as a social body' (ibid.). The choice of how to move thus suddenly lost its supposedly artistic and 'intimate' origin.

There are other similar studies dealing with 'confronting' dance techniques through which contemporary dance and even classical ballet are read as 'Western practice'. For example, writing about nationalism and dance in Turkey, Arzu Öztürkmen notes that 'In the winter of 1991, ballerinas of the State Ballet Ensemble of Turkey found a traditional davul (drum) player in their rehearsals. It was the idea of the Minister of Cultural Affairs that the state-sponsored ballet dancers should learn "our national rhythms!"' (Öztürkmen, 2001:139).

Alfirević notes how the idea of 'dance as a "democratic art form", as a form that can "teach" democracy is much present and it can be seen as a trend in the EU policies. It is treated as the most democratic art form, diversity form, form that is socially engaged and corresponds with diverse cultures' (Alfirević, cited in Tanurovska, 2007:44).

Ana Vujanović states that the structural dependency of the local art scene on international sources of funding puts the contemporary dance practitioner in Serbia (whom she marks as an 'Eastern practitioner') in a paradoxical position. She asserts that:

> There is a critical standpoint on the process of contemporary dance influences that come or are 'imported' from 'the West.' So many times in recent years I have heard complaints by local dance practitioners from Tallinn to Skopje that the only dance practised in the East that is supported both locally and internationally, is the one created under the strong influence of Western contemporary dance, conceptual dance in particular. On the other hand, Eastern choreographers who make their works in the current line of contemporary European dance scene are used to being blamed by Western programmers and critics of lacking anything specifically Eastern. (Vujanović, 2007)

Bojana Kunst (2002) also describes the relationship between the 'Western gaze' and newly 'discovered' Eastern European dance scenes. Thus, she states that the West is not ready to observe Eastern bodies as autonomous, articulated bodies. Eastern dance bodies are, rather, articulated as confused, clumsy, old-fashioned, and romantic. Above all, those bodies are not 'contemporary' and, consequently, their dance is still not 'contemporary'. They are still 'not there' (ibid., 2002). Eastern bodies always enter Western European art scenes as 'spectacular commodities', by communicating either exotic or 'embarrassing' difference. They never appear without a tag of the embarrassing history of socialism or some exotic Balkan flavour of war and trauma. However, Kunst adds that dance from the East was playing the same game. She reports how, during the war in former Yugoslavia, several Slovenian groups managed to successfully 'sell' the 'Balkan context' of their practice although they were coming from completely different backgrounds (ibid.). Slovenia is perhaps an interesting example of the 'least Balkan' Balkan state. Having stepped out from the Balkan quagmire at the beginning of the war, and being comparatively richer than other Yugoslav states, Slovenia had a relatively painless transition, silently joining the EU. Leaving behind any Balkan stigmatization, paradoxically, Slovenia was the first to embrace the 'burden' of the Balkans in certain spaces of artistic production. With war sweeping across the rest of the former Yugoslavia, accompanied by devastating economic conditions and sealed borders, contemporary dance (or any dance) hardly had a chance to develop; yet at the same time, according to the Slovenian theorist Rok Vevar, the Slovenian dance scene was going through some kind of Renaissance. He recalls how

> After highly politicized situation in Yugoslavia of the 1980s, contemporary dance and theatre scene in the 1990s witnessed a huge outburst of creativity and production ... Because of the war in Yugoslavia, foreign producers found Slovenia dance and theatre groups suddenly very attractive in the 1990s. That's why some of them toured the

whole world with their performances. Foreign producers were constantly forcing them into the context of dance and theatre from the war zone, although you can hardly consider Slovenia to be ever in the beginning of the 1990s a war zone. (Vevar, cited in Tanurovska, 2007:49)

A clarification is needed here. Already in the former Yugoslavia, Slovenia had a relatively advanced cultural and avant-garde scene, especially in relation to other republics. So this outburst of creativity might also be a result of the sudden openness of that relatively small scene towards European artistic centres, although as Kunst and Vevar observed, 'war at close quarters' probably influenced and fostered the process. It is not my question here which of these two assumptions is the correct one. The question is not even if Slovenia is indeed a 'Balkan' state. What is important to stress here is that the Slovenian/Balkan example represents the new political logic of contemporary multiculturalism as an appropriation of differences. Slovenia is, thus, allowed to enter the 'European family' as the Balkan state without Balkan negativities; Balkan exotica without Balkan violence and poverty. In this case we can observe the mechanism of 'Othering' by which 'othering can take place by acts of inclusion within multicultural discourse' (Ang 1996, cited in Ahmed, 2000:97).

In this section, I have been outlining the historical and political conditions that shaped the emergence of contemporary dance practices in South East Europe. Contemporary dance practices were, thus, seen as artistic practices with democracy-building potential in the totalitarian, violence-ridden societies. In the following remaining sections, I will introduce my fieldwork methodology and two main points of entrance into dance under globalization.

3. Methodology

My methodological approach is standard anthropological participant-observation inherent to fieldwork analysis. As for the choice of ethnographic fieldwork, I had difficulties in conceptualizing the location of my research. Initially, I wanted to write about South East Europe and the people, male dancers in this case, that are produced by, but also that actively produce this social and political 'place'. However, soon it became obvious that defining South East Europe is not an easy endeavour: as a term it is a relatively loose and new way of naming the countries that were known as both the Balkans and Eastern Europe simultaneously. Finally, I decided to search for informants from countries that were historically, at some point, part of the Ottoman Empire — Turkey, Serbia, Romania, and Macedonia. In anthropology, it seems to me, such an act of choosing one's fieldwork always already assumes a set of personal, political, or even material choices. Likewise, the research is never conducted in some sort of sterile scientific environment but it always assumes a dialogue between at least two persons with different backgrounds and agendas.

The identity of the researcher in fieldwork and reflexivity in ethnographic writing has been one of the major concerns of postmodern anthropology (Marcus, 1995; Ortner, 1984). Stoeltje, Fox, and Olbrys describe academic research in the postcolonial world metaphorically:

> Entering a culture to carry out ethnographic research, whether it is familiar or strange to the ethnographer, is much like looking into a pool of water. Depending on the light and time of the day, one may see a reflection of oneself, refracted perhaps because of the ripples on the surface. At sunset the reflection of the surrounding trees

and foliage appear, and eventually one sees deeply into the water, simultaneously becoming aware of the underwater world, the forest, the sunlight, and one's own reflection. (Stoeltje, Fox, and Olbrys, 1999:159)

These authors underline that anthropological research is increasingly concerned with the reflexivity of the researcher in addressing issues such as history and power in post-coloniality. As a Serbian 'outside anthropologist' pursuing a PhD and later working at a UK university, I found my research brought me to a familiar 'home-like' terrain, and as a result I expected that I would have fewer obstacles in defining and understanding the different contexts of my research. Archetti, however, warns us that the '"inside" perspective in auto-anthropology is not necessarily that of the "natives"'(Archetti, 1999:xiv). I tried to bear this in mind especially when working in Serbia.

The major part of this research was carried out in different periods from 2008 through to 2009, during which I travelled to several countries to conduct interviews or simply to spend some time with the dancers in question, watching them perform, rehearse, or run workshops. As mentioned in the previous chapter, I focused my study on four male dancers, but I also included numerous other dancers, cultural workers, and managers in this study. I have conducted my research through formal interviews, informal conversations, and observations. In the remaining chapters the voice of these dancers will be very prominent, and I have included only the information dancers allowed me to. The interviews with Turkish and Romanian dancers were conducted in English; with Serbian dancers, they were conducted in the Serbian language; and with Macedonian dancers we spoke Serbian/Macedonian respectively and were able to communicate with each other. Finally, as this book is being published over a research period of several years, I was challenged and forced to re-examine some of the findings, and to note subtle but existing changes between 2008 and 2013 on international and local dance scenes. The final fieldwork on this book was conducted in September 2013 in Belgrade, when I included final material and gained a fresh perspective and again was faced with the fact that small, almost imperceptible shifts did take place. These shifts will be noted duly.

Interviews: The concept and questions for the interviews were basically the same for all dancers, except for some specific questions connected with their biographies. I found Michael Gard's book *Men Who Dance, Aesthetic, Athletic and the Art of Masculinity* (Gard, 2006) extremely helpful for structuring the interviews. Gard's work on dance and masculinity was important in obtaining a general idea of the way the phenomenon of dance can be addressed by pointing to the issue of subjectivity and pleasure from the perspectives of dancers themselves and consequently highlighting the significance of fieldwork. Although Gard's main concerns lay within gender studies and dance education, the way he organized the interviews was very helpful in building a meaningful and more or less linear structure for the interviews. The general structure I followed in the interviews was as follows:

— Childhood and beginnings: In which the dancers were invited to introduce their families, social positioning, the environment of their childhood, their home town, and the local dance/performance practice scenes. This part also addressed their first memories of dance, their first dance experiences and the social consequences of their decisions to become dancers/performers.

— Development of dance practice and significant works: This was the most important part of the interviews, inviting the dancers to reflect on the development of their practices, their most important works, as well as the connection between their practices and their sexuality and private lives. This part was differentiated to a large extent among dancers, as it was organized according to their biographies as well as according to specific theoretical points posed in the book.

— A third part was organized as a reflection on different theoretical topics. The dancers were invited to address the issue of dance in general through questions such as: What is dance? Who is a 'good' dancer? and so on. Under the rubric of home, organized around the question What is home?, we addressed issues of national/ethnic/regional identification. With regard to the topic of audiences and critics, the dancers were invited to speak about critics' and audiences' responsiveness and the way this influences their works.

My research combines stories and histories told by the informants with a historical and material analysis of the contexts in which these stories emerge and produce meanings. Significant space was dedicated to different 'narratives' told by the informants—narratives born out of experience but also giving shape to that experience (see Ochs and Capps, 1996). I use 'narrative' here in the way Ochs and Capps understand it: it implies both subjects/selves as discrete entities and 'selves in terms of others in present, past, and imagined universes' (ibid:29). That is why I include significant direct quotations from my informants themselves. While the contextual analysis of these accounts is in most cases mine, my intention is to 'colour' the analysis with the personal voices of the dancers as much as possible, because these personal colourings, in the end, shape the everyday practices I am addressing and which I can only partially access myself. This is important to stress as this aspect of my research differs from the common anthropological analysis in which informants remain to a degree anonymous. Since I have only four informants on whose close and longstanding collaboration this book relies, I found it necessary for their voices to be present as much as possible. However, I believe that there are many things left 'untold', and that this kind of research can be and must be understood through careful and tireless contextualization. To conclude I will invoke Žižek's assertion that, after all, knowing the 'Other' is an ontological problem and not only an epistemological concern (Žižek, 1997:50-1). Thus my investigation of South East European contemporary dance will offer, in general, a perspective on dance studies as a historically Western discipline being explored through other, not completely Western spaces. This will involve a focus on the following two dimensions.

Firstly, my investigation will offer a new perspective on a much discussed issue in dance studies — that of gender in theatrical dance. In particular, I address the paradox of the 'man who dances' (Gard, 2006) in societies which are often deemed the last bastions of patriarchy in Europe (see Ramet, 1999).

The second dimension in my research will be the question of dance and labour or dancer's labour. The investigation of labour in dance studies has occurred mostly through a discussion of dance in relation to labour movements (Graff, 1997; Franko, 2002; Morris, 2006) and/or national politics (Martin, 1998). I address this question starting from a discussion of more global changes in the regime of work under the dominance of communication industries and service work (Hardt and Negri, 2000) and the consequences of this change for dancers. The dancer will be discussed as a paradigmatic example of the 'immaterial worker'. I will further relate this question to the yet unresolved split between mind work and body work in dance. This question, I would argue, gained some urgency within recent discussions about the methodology of analysis in dance scholarship (Giersdorf, 2009) or the methodology of creating dance/choreography (Spångberg, 2006). The question of the mind/body split of the dancer's labour revolving around the question of conceptual dance is also important for dance scholarship. Giersdorf, for instance, discusses the manual/intellectual split in dance scholarship which occurred through the nineteenth-century and twentieth-century educational systems. He states:

> As all of us in higher education know, this hierarchy between the manual labour of training and the intellectual labour of theorization/historization is much more complex than it appears. We know that training is intellectual labour, and increased attention to the physicality of theoretization has challenged the ephemeral nature of thought. (Giersdorf, 2009:27–8)

Although dance scholarship gradually asked questions about its own methodology (see Adshead, 1988; Foster, 1986; 1996a) the complexity of the mind body/split in dance (studies) still persists. I address this complexity through the question of the dancer's labour. However, rather than focusing on the problem of dance spectatorship and theoretization, I will concentrate on this question from the dancer's point of view, that is, starting from the way this split emerges in everyday practices of dancers. More generally, I will relate these questions back to much older discussions about the body and subjectivity through the specific lenses of the labouring body — the body at work.

In the following three sections, I will discuss the aforementioned dimensions of my work in more detail.

4. Dance and Gender

Anthropological research on the lives of theatrical dancers, dance education and networks is rare. Neither anthropologists nor dance scholars have pursued in-depth research on theatrical dance companies. There appears to be a persistent divide between ethnographic approaches (usually applied to popular, non-European, or folk dances) and aesthetical approaches favoured by dance scholars (usually applied to elite and/or Eurocentric dance forms). Many sustained studies of dancers and the dance world that include interviewing dancers about their career experiences, have come from dance education scholars who had an experience of or interest in teaching. These studies are predominantly aimed at understanding the motives that young people have in pursuing dance careers (Stinson, Blumenfeld-Jones, and van Dyke, 1990) and to some extent to make some improvements in dance education that, over the years, have come under considerable scrutiny. Dance training often involves inhumane treatment of dancers, rigid and insensitive training, idealization of particular body types that produces rampant eating disorders, drug use among dancers, and verbal and sexual harassment of dancers from those in position of power (Risner, 2002; Gordon, 1984). A number of these studies concentrated on the issue of gender in dance education, focusing on the experiences of female dancers (Green, 1999; Stinson, Blumenfield-Jones, and van Dyke, 1990), and pointing to the relationship between gender and the experience of dance and dance education.

The problem of gender representation and female agency in theatrical dance, especially ballet, has been thoroughly discussed by feminist and dance scholars (Daly, 1987; Banes, 1998; Burt, 1995; Albright, 1990, 1997, 1998; Case et al., 1995; Thomas, 1993; Foster, 1996a; Shapiro, 1998). Although Western theatrical dance underwent serious historical changes that made possible a more 'democratic' dance body (Banes, 1994), the problem of the 'perfect dance body' persists. Jill Green's study 'Somatic Authority and the Myth of the Ideal Body in Dance Education' (1999) offers in-depth research with a few female dancers with names and personal histories. Green investigates how the body is shaped by society and the dance world in which dancers risk health and identity problems as they constantly strive for perfection. Green deliberately focuses her research on the body of the female dancer arguing that it is under considerably more pressure than that of the male dancer: female dancers experience more hardships than their male colleagues during the training and later while building up a career. Reading studies dealing with the experiences of female dancers, one gets a strong impression that differences in experiences between female and male dancers may be shockingly large. It is worth considering, however, that studies of male dance experiences are virtually non-existent.

Risner (2002) explores the experience of gay male dancers in dance education, questioning the absence of the scholarly literature on gay and bisexual men in dance although, according to him, they comprise half of the male population in dance. Acknowledging the literature on dance and masculinity, Risner remains predominantly interested in the social analysis of the 'homophobic myths' that are cultivated in dance education and which account for the hardships of gay male dancers during their training. There are two significant issues raised by Risner's study. Firstly, his conclusions on the experience of gay male dancers are at odds with the studies of female experiences of dance training. Addressing gender differences in experiences of dance education, Risner asserts that 'Boys in dance, unlike their male peers in athletic and team sports, are participating in an activity that already sheds social suspicion on their masculinity and heterosexuality. Alternatively, dance for young girls affirms their femininity and buttresses the image of heterosexual orientation' (Risner, 2002:68).

These sound theoretical assertions cannot however adequately address the different experience of male and female dancers in dance education. Green's research indicated a somewhat different story, pointing to a greater pressure on female dance bodies, severe competition among female dancers and fewer career choices than male dancers. The reason is that disproportionally larger numbers of girls are entering dance education, but it is also worth remembering that the majority of choreographers, directors, and dance educators are male (Burt, 1995).

A second important issue regarding Risner's study is whether his findings address experiences of male dancers in general, or only those of gay dancers. Risner explicitly talks almost exclusively about the experience of homosexual dancers in dance education, but he relies heavily on literature on masculinity and dance, which points out, that the stigma of homosexuality applies to any male dancer, since Western theatrical dance bears the assumption of homosexuality.

In *The Male Dancer: Bodies, Spectacle, Sexualities* (1995) Ramsay Burt theoretically elaborates on issues of dance and masculinity, providing a rich and critical exploration of the cultural, social, political, and economic history of masculine representation in Western theatrical dance. He concentrates on the twentieth-century construction of prejudice towards male dancers and on the homophobia that surrounds male dancers. Following Sedgwick (1985, cited in Gard, 2006) and Bristow (1988, cited in Gard, 2006), Burt claims that homophobia related to male dancers was developed as a means for males to rationalize their attraction to one another. Burt further argues that the crux for the heterosexual male spectatorship watching men dance is precisely straddling the important boundary for men—that between acceptable homosocial bonding and repressed homosexual attraction.

Although Burt's study is significant in theoretical terms, Michael Gard's *Men Who Dance, Aesthetic, Athletic & Art of Masculinity* (2006) is the most illuminating contribution to the field, offering both a theoretical standpoint on dance and masculinity and a practical exploration of male dancers' identities. Gard's main interest is in the question of how males become theatrical dancers. He starts from the assumption that becoming male is a kind of a 'project', thus tackling questions of sexuality and masculinity, and then proceeds to argue that becoming a man who dances is a 'particular kind of project' that has certain 'rules'. Through an exploration of these 'rules' one can address more complex issues: that of male sexuality and that of the nature of dance. A particularly significant aspect of Gard's research (and in this it differs from Burt's research) is its methodology. Gard conducted a number of in-depth interviews with male dancers, allowing the readers to 'peer into' the dance world from the particular position of male dancers themselves.

Let me single out two important consequences of this methodological approach that are particularly instructive for my research. Firstly, interviews provide good examples of the retrospective construction of life and identity that is in process, situated in several overlapping contexts (historical, cultural, and biographical). Secondly, this methodology allows us to dwell on the ways these dancers talk about their private lives, career choices, dance aesthetics, anecdotes, fears, and desires which could reveal not only their pleasure in dancing but also their pleasure in being. Gard is especially keen on addressing the issue of pleasure in dance reminding us that the 'specificity' of dance resides not only in its embodied nature but also in the fact that dancers usually feel pleasure in moving (Gard, 2006). This aspect of dance is often approached through the notion of kinaesthetics. Gard, however, considers this problematic and suggests that the experience and pleasure of dancing cannot be divorced from the socially mediated circulation of meanings about dance and the investment that people have in being particular kinds of (dancing) subjects. Certainly, pleasure is not the only sensation that can be connected to certain subject positions. Uncertainty and fear are also worth acknowledging. Gard's specific interest in pleasure derives from Hollway's theory of gender formation and 'investments'. Hollway addresses the notion of 'investment' in certain (heterosexual) gender positions in discourses of sexuality. She explains how sexuality discourses that put female sexuality in opposition and subordination to male sexual drive discourse, offer certain kinds of power and certain kinds of pleasure to both women and men. Gard uses Hollway's theory of investments in certain subject positionings (even the ones that put the subject in a subordinate position), clarifying that 'Without theorizing the tension produced in constructing gender subjectivities, we are left with the appearance of an unproblematic process with an inevitable outcome' (ibid.:20).

While I share Gard's concerns regarding the process of gender creation and identification, my research will not address it, as his does, through the theoretical discussion of subjectivity. Instead, I propose to discuss the different workings of Western conceptualizations of masculinity and dance in the social, political, and theoretical contexts of South East Europe. My research will depart from Gard's not only on this methodological level, but in theoretical terms. Gard uses Sparkes's (1999, cited in Gard, 2006) notion of 'body stories' to address narratives about men's embodied experiences of dance and to construct a discussion of 'investments' in different subject positionings. My research is not organized around body stories, although I concur with Gard's notion that dance studies should depart from interpreting pleasure in moving solely in kinaesthetic terms and address social contexts that define that pleasure. Two of the dancers I focus on embraced a conceptual dance aesthetic, more or less rejecting movement, and 'body stories' did not figure much in their accounts. This fact drew me further away from considering dance as an 'event of moving', accompanied by intense physical training, towards addressing it as a field of cultural production, in Bourdieu's sense (1993), with its own history, actors, and struggles over legitimization and power. Finally, let me highlight one more difference between Gard's and my own research, which is related to the social and ethnic backgrounds of the dancers we study and which probably greatly influenced our research trajectories. Gard's dancers are coming from white and mostly middle class backgrounds, and as he points out himself: 'the fact that stories about overcoming sexist or racist prejudice or economic hardship did not figure prominently in their accounts tells us something about the backgrounds of the dancers and the kind of profession theatrical dance is' (Gard, 2006:168). Although this may be true for theatrical dance in Australia, my examples point to a somewhat different picture for the societies in which I carried out my research. Stories about ethnic or racial prejudices, wars, social unrest, and economic hardship figure greatly in the accounts of the dancers I studied. Perhaps that is why my interest was rather in what Gard refers to as the sociology of dance, rather than in the construction of identities, which was Gard's primary concern (ibid.:167–8). Nevertheless, Gard seems right to point out that, even with similar backgrounds, there is no 'biographical "formula" which leads to the answer "male theatrical dancer"'(ibid.). As Judith Lynne Hanna (1987) asserts: a male dancer was always a special kind of minority.

5. Dance as Labour and Production

In recent times the economy of the western world has been transformed dramatically from a Fordist model to a new, postindustrial one. As authors such as Linda McDowell (2009) have shown, for a growing number of individuals entering the wage labour market this has involved an evident change in working conditions compared to those of previous workers, especially those of manufacturing industries. This change is the key motif of recent theoretical discussions on waged work, termed 'new capitalism', 'post-Fordism', 'liquid modernity', etc. (ibid.). Whatever term is used, a basic feature of this change consists of a switch from the manufacturing economy of the past to the service economy of the present.

According to Hardt and Negri, immaterial labour is labour that produces immaterial goods, such as a service, a cultural product, or communication. In this sense, they identify the postindustrial economy as an informational economy insofar as: 'The jobs for the most part are highly mobile and involve flexible skills ... they are characterized by the central role played by knowledge, information, affect, and communication' (Hardt and Negri, 2000:285). Similarly, according to Dirlik 'the new worker [that is] modelled after the symbolic-analyst is a closer approximation of the pre-capitalist artisan who has far greater control over product, and the process of production' (Dirlik, 1998:197).

Sally Gardner questions 'dance-making' relations of production between dancer and choreographer and the way in which this relation has been conceived or 'imagined' through conceptual tools of dance scholarship. She states that aesthetic modernism and dance scholarship conceived dancer-choreographer relations through a strict division of labour (choreography vs dancing). This aesthetic division can be further elucidated in terms of industrial modernity:

> The difficulty for aesthetic modernism of conceiving the choreographer and the dancer other than as a division of labour (choreography vs dancing) can be further elucidated by repositioning this aesthetic division within the terms of industrial modernity: that is by linking the ideology of the disembodied 'work of art' to a particular, dominant mode of economic production. ... The idea of 'production' arising as it does within capitalism, suggests a subsuming of several arts within a totality controlled and directed from the position outside of those arts. (Gardner, 2007:40)

If, following Gardner, we conclude that modernist thought had difficulties in conceiving of choreographer and dancer other than within a division of labour, we may ask what the situation with postmodern thought is. Gardner, in fact, claims that modern thought privileged the finished product—a 'work of art' (which in terms of dance would be the choreography)—against a process of production (intersubjective and intercorporeal relationships between dancer and choreographer in the process of creating dance).

We can see from Lepecki's project (2006b), described in Chapter One that dancers/choreographers are now working on dismantling a stable product of dance, i.e. choreography. Instead, there is an emphasis on the process—intercorporeal relations between dancers and choreographer, dancers and audience … We can say that the research into this relationship is the primary interest for dancers, as they move from working on dance productions/pieces towards dance projects. Similarly, dance scholarship exemplified by Lepecki is not interested in describing and then analyzing a dance piece, as choreography disappears as such. Instead, dance scholarship writes about the process/project: What was a choreographer's initial idea? Who was involved in a project and how? What is a choreographer's theoretical/philosophical background in which he/she grounds his/her practice? How was the rehearsal process conducted from day one?, and so on.

The actual dance performance as such (the project outcome) is the least important as the project is not designed to produce a performance, but the very project is performance, and the project/performance is life itself. We can relate this to the way in which Luc Boltanski and Ève Chiapello define the 'new spirit of capitalism' as project-oriented, defined through activity rather than through 'work'. This 'activity' cannot stand for traditionally conceived work since it is oriented precisely towards dismantling the opposition between work and leisure, but it can be only understood as life itself. Life which is conceived as a series of projects:

> What is relevant is to be always pursuing some sort of activity, never to be without a project, without ideas, to be always looking forward to, and preparing for, something along with other persons whose encounter is the result of being always driven by the impulse of activity. (Boltanski and Chiapello, 2005:169)

Marina Gržinić sees in this insistence on artistic creativity rather than on a finished product the profound relationship between contemporary arts and the biopolitical production of life itself. She states that:

> There is a process of subjectification at work today in the field of contemporary artistic production which does not take place through work, but through artistic creativity, the latter redefines precisely, or, if you want, colonizes what work is. The production and instrumentalization of life (what is known as biopolitics) become in such a context (of a redefinition of labour) of a fundamental importance for capital. (Gržinić, 2009)

Dance also found itself in the midst of the changes in 'artistic work' and modes of labour. Bojana Bauer connects changes in European choreography during the 1990s, with the shift in work, following the dismantling of stable companies which precipitated a 'lot of talk about the socio-economic status of independent performing artists' (Bauer, 2008:15). She continues: 'Multiplying not only projects but statuses and positions as well, and exceeding the frames of what is defined as "work", the independent artist is most often identified as the paradigmatic exponent of immaterial labour' (ibid.:16). Similarly, Pouillaude discusses changes in European dance practice identifying features of 'mutation': 'The first feature consists of the dissolution of fixed companies. The team of stable and salaried collaborators — what one formerly called "company" is replaced by temporary local coalitions, individuals handling their own artistic careers in an autonomous way, gathering around a defined project' (Pouillaude, 2007:131).

He claims, however, that this intermittence is no longer something we should lament, as, according to him it was not due to economic factors. Thus, 'the regime of intermittence is not a compensation for an ideal salary-earning situation that everyone should strive to reach; rather it simply accompanies, at a social level and in an absolutely essential way, a liberation fully assumed by the actors' (ibid.). Pouillaude seems to claim that the socio-economic change of status of artists simply followed their own desires for change. However, soon he adds that:

> The main punch lies in the play of parentheticals: once the 'artistic' parenthetical is eliminated, what is it that remains but a formulation of MEDEF's economic program?[12] This mutation of dance's labour is not without consequences for the very concept of the work (oeuvre). (Ibid.)

So Pouillade clearly indicates that a particular dance aesthetic also depends on the way a dancer's labour is economically recognized and organized. Following Menger

---

[12] MEDEF, Mouvement des Enterprises de France (Movement of French Enterprises) is the largest association of employers in France (Pouillaude, 2007:131).

(2002), he clearly sees a connection between the 'liberal mutation of arts of spectacle (arts du spectacle)' and a 'general precariousness of labour within the "ordinary" economy' (Menger, 2002, cited in Pouillaude, 2007).

D'Amelio (2008) explains the inclination of contemporary French choreographers to explore philosophical concepts in their work in a similar manner, arguing that the emergence of a particular dance aesthetic (termed 'Nondance') can be partly understood through the mutual dependence of dance and state funding. She states that:

> The way in which funding is applied for and distributed may also be fostering the conceptual turn of French contemporary dance. Civil servants looking over a choreographer's grant application may not know how to 'read' choreography, but they may have read Barthes, for example, and this is shared culture on which aspiring choreographers can call. Neither does dance scholarship escape this circle of mutually constituting influences. (D'Amelio, 2008:100)

The particular 'conceptual turn' in French dance,[13] D'Amelio also explains with the fact that theatres in France are heavily subsidized by the state and that artists generally enjoy 'greater economic stability relative to those working in other European countries' providing them 'with a measure of artistic freedom not enjoyed elsewhere' (ibid.:93).

Many dancers are also aware of material and labour conditions that shape their dance practices. Xavier Le Roy

---

[13] Unlike Lepecki and Pouillaude, D'Amelio localizes the 'new turn in contemporary dance' to a particular French avant-garde scene. Notwithstanding the difference in understanding, the dance phenomenon they all describe is the same.

openly admits the role of 'economy' in the production and perception of his dance work. Thus, when asked in an interview to reflect on his relationship with the reproduction of his most shown piece 'Self Unfinished', he answered:

> First of all, its business isn't it? My relation to reproduction is business. It's about economics. Maybe a bit cynical answer but according to what makes a piece repeated, it is part of it...It's the way I live. ... To reproduce the piece, more precisely to repeat it, I got money. .. Its one form of exchange which is at stake in this situation. [sic, reproduced as in original] (Le Roy, n.d.)

Le Roy is not the only artist making a statement on the production and reproduction of art work within the art market of capitalism. In fact, we could say that the exploration of and comments on the market value of arts appear as integral parts of many art productions as such. Le Roy, however, may be unique in that he explicitly acknowledges the consequence of the change of labour within dance for dance practice as such. He admits that when he started thinking about a dance career (he is also a professional biologist) he was attracted to the very idea of dance work, which was very different from the work of the biologist in a laboratory. To him,

> it meant somehow a confusion between the idea of leisure time and working time, another role and a different mode of living which I imagined being a different understanding of the society [but later] I realized that actually this mode of life made of activities where the border between work, leisure, productive, unproductive are confused, became a mode of life imposed by the transformation and the development of what Luc Boltanski and Ève Chiapello call the 'new spirit of capitalism'. [sic] (Le Roy n.d.)

Thus, remembering his beginnings as a dancer, he continues that:

> We are not more or less involved in the production of something to enter the exchange market we are the producers of ourselves as a product. This kind of new norm is pretty close what I wanted 12 years ago when I did the big jump to resist to a system. Some of these concepts are also close to ideas that I would usually use and defend. But if this is actually imposed to us and not a choice, then it is difficult to defend and practice. [*sic*] (Le Roy, n.d.)

Le Roy is thus aware of the paradox that the new form of capitalism conceptualizes life precisely as an artistic creativity/activity, so that it is extremely difficult to form a critique of capitalism through an art medium. The reason for this is twofold. Firstly, we have seen that the mutual reinforcement of the art and criticism is not a new phenomenon; what is new, however, is the figure of the 'creative worker' and 'creative industry' which makes these interrelations novel and more complex (Pang, 2009) under the 'new spirit of capitalism'. Secondly and consequently the power of the new culture industry is to absorb even the most opposed art forms (Aronowitz, 1994). This situation, as Aronowitz concludes, forces 'the artist to produce work in the context of the requirements of the industry. Or alternatively, the artist remains ostensibly outside it, but is still connected by means of her or his increasing compulsion to comment upon it in the work of art' (ibid.:49).

Aronowitz, thus, clearly underlines that conveyed criticism is already commoditified and absorbed and that artists should be searching for and developing new forms of critical resistance.

Dance, however, holds a specific fascination for the theorists interested in challenging the 'new spirit of capitalism'. Philosophers fascinated with theatricality, from Kierkegaard and Nietzsche, to theorists of performativity of literature and performance studies, speak of a new priority of theatricality and performativity over ontology and essence (Puchner, 2002:521). Gilles Deleuze (1994) uses theatre as a model for his theory of singular events — events that form a series of differences that cannot be reduced to a stabilizing identity behind them. Alain Badiou (2005) following Spinoza understands dance as a metaphor for thought — thinking without relation that does not represent anything but a pure possibility of what the body is capable of. To Badiou, dance is not the child of politics and state (Badiou, 2005:71). Dance scholars were certainly exploring possibilities of thinking about dancing bodies in a Deleuzian fashion by which affective faculties of the human body are seen as a perfect tool for creating immanent democracy based on embodied nature of ethic (Briginshaw and Burt, 2009). Already introduced, through the work of Andrew Hewitt (2005), it became clear that this critical vitalism that emerged in the nineteenth century is consonant with the capitalist ideology of disembodied work and pure production. Despite this fact, Hewitt nevertheless stresses that dance still deserves our attention since dance as an aesthetic medium constantly seeks to understand art as something immanently political. Following the same paradox of thinking about and understanding political potential of dance, Tyson Lewis, along with Hewitt, concludes that:

> dance is a space of indistinction between the actual and the potential ... it is neither labour nor not-labour, it is neither work nor not-work, and it is neither speech nor not speech

... dance contains all of above within itself as a potential to be or not to be. (Lewis, 2007:64)

In Chapter Four I will, thus, return to the question of the political immanence of dance through the discussion of ballet and modern dance techniques under the framework of dance labour. This chapter will address the question of the totality of dance labour by looking at dancers as highly mobile agents of flexible capitalism. In considering the systemic conditions that limit and constrain mobility, it is necessary to take into account the subject's (dancer's) profile in terms of class, gender, and race/nationality in relation to circuits of mobility that include him/her (D'Andrea, 2007). I will argue that even relatively free-flowing metropolitan subjects of globalization, such as artists, business people, and various expatriates, stumble on economic and ethnocentric orientations that condition and constrain their movements. This shift from the political potential of dance to the work, life, and mobility patterns of professional dancers as agents of globalization, will re-emphasize the question of a dancer's body labour under the contemporary ideologies of disembodied, information-centred capitalism (McCarren, 2003).

What happens to the dancing body with the rise of 'cognitive capitalism'? What happens with the energy of the working body, its possibilities and expenditures, its labour-power in the new ideology of disembodied work? These are the questions that will be opened up through the discussion of dance and labour.

As with other chapters, this one will be coloured by personal narratives of my dancers testifying mainly to the specific living and especially working patterns under the new condition of capitalism. As creative, immaterial workers, dancers' narratives will distinguish between ballet technique perceived as a predominantly repetitive physical labour, whereas contemporary dance appears as a creative endeavour. Finally, dancers' narratives will be especially revealing for thinking about globalization in the Western peripheries. Hardt and Negri (2000), in a way, mark this tendency of Empire to constitute itself as an idea of a globalizing, borderless world and at the same time, paradoxically, to keep identifying various 'Others' that are threatening its borders. Thus the

> Empire is emerging today as the center that supports the globalization of productive networks and casts its widely inclusive net to try to envelop all power relations within its world order — and yet at the same time it deploys a powerful police function against the new barbarians and the rebellious slaves who threaten its order. (Hardt and Negri, 2000:20)

The EU is, perhaps, a paradigmatic example of the way the discourse of the 'borderless Europe' includes processes or border erasure within Europe and, at the same time, closure and building up borders to the outside. These mutually existing processes are crucial to our understanding of art practices as immaterial labour in countries that form the EU's 'immediate outside' (Jansen, 2009). On the one hand there is Europe as a notion of a borderless world (with free-floating capital, information, artistic creativity, and collaboration) and on the other hand, we find that Europe's borders are real—they are boundaries creating privileged and non-privileged subjects and subjectivities. Thus, the investigation of South East European dancers as immaterial workers will address the process of overcoming the 'borders within' in the practice of networking and artistic collaborations anticipated by globalization and the new regime of work described by Hardt and Negri. However, this process will be situated in the context of the actual existing external borders since my research was conducted during the time when most South East European countries were still Europe's 'immediate outside'. Chapter Four, then, along with others, traces the shapes of the process of globalization and how it operates within and in relation to the still persistent 'sedentary logic of the state' (D'Andrea, 2007).

CHAPTER 3

GENDER AND MASCULINITIES IN THE WORLD OF CONTEMPORARY PROFESSIONAL DANCE

1. Introduction

> Some people say that the performance is impressive because there are eight male dancers on the stage ... that power makes something ... So if you ask yourself why, you will realise that actually the power of these eight men that are so different body-wise, technique-wise .. makes the whole piece powerful; it is not about steps or staging, it is simply eight men on the stage ... it creates special energy. (Ziya Azazi, 2008b, when asked to comment about the production 'D'Orient' by Belgian based Company Thor in which he performed)
>
> I was not simply asking a group of people how they became dancers, but rather how they, as males, became dancers. (Gard, 2006:46)

Men who dance are ambiguous creatures—simultaneously empowered and marginalized, admired and ridiculed, always in the process of 'negotiation of power and prestige' (Cowan, 1990:189). In writing about the history of masculine representation in Western theatrical dance, Ramsay Burt claims that the dominant attitudes towards men who dance arise from more deeply entrenched modernist attitudes toward the male body and behaviour. Burt opens his discussion with the caption from a nineteenth-century lithograph—'the unpleasant thing about a danseuse is that she sometimes brings along a male dancer' (Burt, 1995:10)—pointing at the status of a male dancer as an 'unpleasant contradiction' and a mere, 'invisible' support for a ballerina. A century has passed since the publication of this caption—a century that allowed a contradistinction between these attitudes and Ziya's claim about a 'special power of dancing male bodies' (Azazi, 2008b). Thus, although 'modern dance and ballet are progressively purifying themselves of outmoded and extraneous representational practices' (Burt, 1995:8), men are still disproportionally the well-recognized choreographers and directors, while women are 'just' dancers and workers. Therefore, men who dance are still rare and their stories may significantly reveal dominant social and gender constructions in professional dance and the wider society. That is why it is important to explore discursive resources male dancers employ to construct themselves and their histories.

This chapter asks the four dancers to tell the stories of their dance beginnings. In doing so, it explores case histories of my dancers and historical moments that relate to dance and masculinities. Unlike Gard's research agenda, this chapter does not aim to explicitly problematize the sex and sexual orientation of the dancers. Instead, I simply asked my dancers to tell the 'story' of how they became dancers from the 'beginning' and let them decide what to emphasize as important and/or decisive. Sexuality and sexual preference did not came forward as important in these narratives, which is odd given that dance scholarship has a long and productive tradition of interest in sexuality of (dancing) bodies (Desmond, 2001; Stoneley, 2007; Hanna, 1988). In this chapter, however, sexual orientation of the dancers seems surprisingly irrelevant. What emerges as relevant is their geopolitical and to a lesser extent class location. That is why this chapter took a specific form of reading the history of masculinities in Western theatrical dance (history of prejudices and 'dangers' connected to male dancers) against personal histories and stories of the selected dancers. In what follows, I seek to expand notions of what can count as theory and what can be counted as dance methodology by using what the anthropologist Dorinne Kondo (1990) calls 'the evocative voice'. The evocative voice, according to Kondo, can indicate the possibilities and limitations involved in the process during which researchers and people in their 'fields' can seek 'to understand each other within shifting fields of power and meaning' (Kondo, 1990:8). To achieve this I left significant portions of the narratives 'uncut' not only to provide a better understanding of that which is being said, but also to evoke that which has not been said — a backdrop or 'stage' of all these narratives: dance and gender in South East Europe and the Middle East in the late twentieth- and the beginning of the twenty-first century.

2. Gender in the History of Western Theatrical Dance

> When a woman dances, nobody cares ... All women can dance. But when a man dances, now that's something. (Perron and Woodard, 1976 cited in Hanna, 1987:42)
>
> There's good news and bad news [about being a man in ballet]. The good news is you're gonna stand out, and that's the bad news. The bad news is you're gonna stand out. (male dancer cited in Hamera, 2007:123)

It is generally argued that, in its beginnings, ballet was predominantly, although not entirely, a male preserve (Gard, 2006:46; see also Au, 1988; Hanna, 1987). As Susan Au (1988) observes, in the Italian and French courts during the Middle Ages and the Renaissance, dance was mostly a male, aristocratic endeavour, often led by a king or a queen and those dancers of the earliest ballets were far removed from the dance professionals of today regarding their technical skills. During the nineteenth century ballet achieved its modern identity by being professionalized, and its 'technical demands' were standardized. Hanna (1987) reports how that change occurred with the French and Industrial Revolutions when the bourgeoisie saw court dances as a source of moral laxity. Under the new regime the body ceased to be an instrument of pleasure and became an instrument of production.

Control over bodily pleasures was an important goal for the bourgeoisie as they avoided engaging in the dance profession. Thus, in the nineteenth century the ultimate and the central figure of ballet was the figure of the ballerina as the ideal of effeminate beauty and 'illusive fragility' (Foster, 1998:11; see also Garafola, 1985). Ballet also ceased to be connected with the aristocracy, at least concerning the class origins of the ballerina. Banes shows that the most celebrated ballerinas of that period were working-class, poorly paid women, who were expected to be sexually available to their wealthy male patrons (Banes, 1998; Hanna, 1987). Male dancers became almost invisible, reduced to the role of dance support for female dancers. Burt (1995) argues that the appearance of male dancers on the 'newly effeminate ballet stage' became a source of anxiety for the bourgeois spectator, because there was no separation between the aesthetic experience of ballet and ballet as an erotic spectacle. Thus, for the bourgeois spectator, to enjoy watching a man dancing was to admit to being sexually interested in men, as the male dancers blurred the line between 'approved homosocial bonding [and] forbidden homosexual sexuality' (Burt, 1995:28).

Gender and Masculinities in Professional Dance

In this period professional male dancers in Europe and America were increasingly assumed to be homosexual. 'Ballet was tagged as the "pansies' ball game" … In Russia, where dancers were recruited as children to audition for government-supported training out of economic necessity, heterosexuality may have been more common' (Hanna, 1987:27).[14] The exception to the rule was thus probably the popularity of the Ballets Russes which reintroduced male dancing and produced during Romanticism the greatest male and female ballet stars, the most popular of them being Vaslav Nijinsky. In explaining why these dance figures, especially Nijinsky, appealed to a wide range of bourgeois and aristocratic, male and female audiences, Burt underlines several reasons. First, Nijinsky's ability to generate dramatic effects through his characters was read as a specific type of male genius, corresponding with the Romantic notion of the artist. The male artist was thus 'excepted from gendered divisions of social behaviour through being allowed to have "feminine" qualities such as sensitivity, passivity, emotionality, and introspective self-consciousness' (Burt. 1995:18). Second, Nijinsky's often gender transgressive appearance and his more or less open homosexuality was often read on Western stages as a trace of the Other: 'uncivilized' and 'wild' Russian culture (as ballet critics of the time often emphasized). Hence, Nijinsky's dance can be seen as a 'spectacle of Otherness' rather than as a spectacle of a man who dances.

---

[14] The professionalization of ballet in Russia is especially interesting not only because of the success of Ballet Russes to redeem the male dancer during Romanticism, but also regarding professional ballet in Soviet Russia and other socialist countries. I will return to this point later.

Soon, however, during the opening decades of the twentieth century, a new form of dance emerged which, once again, restaged gender representation in dance. With the rise of modern dance a new kind of male dancer emerged—athletic, virile, and strong. Many male choreographers of the time, such as Ted Shawn, went to great pains to avoid any assumption of homosexuality, 'uncontrolled' or transgressive sexuality, and to connect theatrical dance with sport.

As Burt rightly observed, rather than the exotic genius of Nijinsky, 'Shawn sought to close the gap between the sportsman and the dancer by equating them and borrowing from sport's by now well established cultural legitimacy as a "maker of men". Rather than challenging the homosexual stereotype he side-stepped it' (Gard, 2006:62; see also Foulkes, 2001). Thus, Gard concludes that the 'new' male dancer was produced on the threshold between the spectacle of the male body as an expressive, embodied artistic genius and the virtuosic, athletic, and disciplined male body. However, central to Gard's argument is that the latter dance figure—the male dancer as the supreme athlete—'has come to occupy the dominant discursive position in constructions of who the male dancer is, and what kinds of skills a male needs to become a professional dancer' (Gard, 2006.:76). Although as the result of this discursive strategy, the number of male dancers increased over time, this does not mean that the assumption of homosexuality connected with male dancers disappeared. Gard's research indeed shows the careful discursive positioning by his dancers regarding their sexual identities and their profession. In that context, note this fieldwork account of the anthropologist Helena Wulff, who conducted an ethnography of three ballet companies in the early 1990s:

Gender and Masculinities in Professional Dance

> Early in my fieldwork study I was having lunch in the canteen with a number of male dancers in the company. They were joking about the erotic side of ballet and 'dancing as a way to keep one's erotic impulses at bay'. Then they became more serious and started to inform me quite assertively, without my having asked about it, 'We are not gay!' They talked about the belief that male dancers are gay while in fact most male dancers in this company were not. They were concerned about this and about making sure I realized that they were 'like any ordinary guys who are interested in technical stuff. The only difference is that we're interested in ballet.' One of them even showed me a picture that he kept in his wallet of his cherished car as a proof of his 'normality', as he phrased it. (Wulff, 1998:113)

Despite the still complicated position that male dancers occupy regarding societal norms of what is a 'respectable' profession for a man, it has frequently been suggested that within the profession gender relations are still in favour of men, thus reflecting, in the end, gender relationships in the wider society. According to Burt, men still hold positions of power in the hierarchically structured dance world. Reading ballet history as a discrete field of gender struggle, Ninette de Valois, choreographer and founding member of England's Royal Ballet, states that:

> Whenever I'm lecturing I always say to people, 'Don't you realise that the history of ballet is the history of the male dancer and the male choreographer?' It has nothing to do with women, except in a secondary role. It's only when the whole thing's come down to nothing that women become the best pioneer workers. They make the best secretaries, for the same reason, but once ballet's got a certain level again it's got to be handed back to the men. (Dominic and Gilbert, 1971, cited in Gard, 2006:64)

Closely connected to this suggestion is the notion, discussed above, that female and male dancers can have completely different experiences of their professional development and perspectives. For instance, a number of the male dancers interviewed by Gard started considering dance as a professional option when they were in their twenties, or even as 'late' as at the age of twenty-seven. Also, three out of the four dancers I worked with, developed both their interest in dance and their dance careers in their twenties. Contrast this with the following remarks of an eighteen-year-old female dancer on her future career prospects: 'I think I could make it in the corps level in New York, but I think I started too late to go any further—not that I couldn't do it but that I'm too old for their standards' (Stinson, Blumenfield-Jones, and van Dyke, 1990:18).

The research from which this quotation is borrowed included female dancers who started dancing from an early age and yet it was found that several girls were already giving up their dreams because in one way or another, they thought they could not succeed in becoming a major performer. Several of the interviewed female dancers in this study indicated that it is easier for men to be successful in dance because there is less competition (ibid.:19). Apparently, a teenage female dancer, after years of hard training, can already anticipate the limits of her future career prospects, while a man can 'discover' dance as a profession and start from the beginning in his late twenties. Such is the case of Laurence, one of the dancers Gard interviewed, who started dancing in his late twenties after another career of many years.

These are, perhaps, extreme examples and my aim is not to suggest that all male dancers work less hard to succeed than their female colleagues. Firstly, Laurence was an exception among Gard's dancers, who usually tended to be engaged in some form of dance from an early age, and some of them even professionally. Secondly, there are areas of dance that do not demand such technical skill and long-term training as ballet, and that are open to more mature and less technically skilled male and female dancers.

All research on dance, we should remember, indicates huge differences in experiences of the dance profession and the training involved among research participants of the same or different sex. As previously noted, Gard implies that there is no one 'type' of man pursuing a dancing career. Nevertheless, certain correlations could be traced among experiences of the dancers I interviewed and also a number of similarities in experiences between the (South East European, Middle Eastern) dancers I worked with and Gard's (Western, Australian) dancers. A significant difference here is connected precisely to the field of gender and sexuality. A number of Gard's dancers encountered different degrees of social disapproval towards their dance profession, connected to the assumption of homosexuality. Many of them were under pressure to conceal their interest in dance until they grew up. None of the dancers I worked with experienced any such pressure, although there are different pressures connected to the dance profession for them too. It sometimes seemed that they were 'blind' to the gender implications of their profession and, when I asked them about this, several did not understand the question or simply did not have anything to say about it. The Macedonian dancer 'Alexander' is the only one who reported that, after he enrolled in dance, there was gossip circulating in his home town Prilep about his alleged homosexuality, but he reported this with a smile, dismissing the whole thing as a 'small town mentality business'.

Although aware of this, it did not affect him personally, socially, or professionally.

Starting from Burt's and Gard's assumption that attitudes towards dancing males reflect gender politics of a certain society, I will, in dialogue with Gard's findings, discuss gender relations and masculinity in the societies that the dancers I worked with originate from. Since Ziya Azazi, Turkish/Arab dancer, is the only dancer coming from a Middle Eastern, capitalist society, I shall begin with his case discussing it somewhat separately from the others. The remaining three dancers will be discussed more or less within the same frame as all of them come from the historically and culturally 'imagined' Balkan region (Todorova, 1997). They grew up during socialism and developed their careers during postsocialist, turbulent and transitory times.

3. Dancing at the Borders of Europe: Ziya Azazi

As with many dancers Gard interviewed, there are no straightforward clues from his childhood to Ziya's eventual career choice. Raised in a small Arab village in the South of Turkey, Ziya was not exposed to ballet or any kind of theatrical dance before moving to Istanbul to study at university. However, much like Laurence, an Australian dancer interviewed by Gard, without being exposed to any theatrical dance forms, Ziya considers his childhood formative to his subsequent dancing career. Laurence grew up in a small Australian town in the early seventies and his memories of his hometown suggest 'idyllic simplicity, far removed from the aesthetic circles he would later inhabit' (Gard, 2006:114). Laurence depicts his birthplace as 'a beautiful place to live in' (ibid.), with its river, mountains, and forests. Ziya also depicts his hometown Antakya with much fondness, recalling its multicultural character and its liveliness. He also refers frequently to the village near Antakya where he spent most of his early years. His father was a tailor and the only provider for this five-member family, and Ziya remembers their one-room house. Admitting that it was a very modest life, he says he never thought of them as being poor. Laurence further stresses the huge importance of social dances (ballroom) in his hometown, when 'everybody danced' (ibid.). He claims that it was the situation in all small Australian towns until 'television and so forth knocked all that on the head' (ibid.:115). Ziya also sees his village isolation and social conformity as supportive and formative for his dance aesthetic. When asked if there were any dancers in his family he replied: 'All the members are dancers. When you make parties or wedding celebrations, you see how everybody dances and they dance for hours' (Azazi, 2008a). Consequently, his first dance memory is connected to a wedding celebration:

> I can remember my first memory is this ... I can't remember very well ... I don't know how old I was. Maybe six, seven, eight ... I don't know ... My mother was wondering: 'who is this boy in the middle of this dancing area and shaking?' And she realized that it was me. And I was telling my mother before the wedding that I'm not interested in celebration and dancing. That was before she had seen her son in the middle of the dancing area shaking away like hell and looking really happy. I can always remember this. ... After this occasion my mother also came to me and said: 'Ah you have been dancing, I saw you' and this memory I have. But like a grey picture moving in my mind. This is the oldest memory that I have. (Ibid.)

That was the only contact Ziya had with dance because he says, other kinds of dances did not exist in Antakya and they did not have a television. Moreover, Ziya reports how he spent the first eighteen years of his life in Antakya and his village, never travelling anywhere else. Growing up 'within twenty-five kilometres' (Azazi, 2008a) was, however, decisive in his earliest body skills:

> We didn't have TV. Dancing has happened to me in a totally different way. ... My first experience was at the village. I was moving, running, climbing on the trees, swimming, working in the garden, playing with the friends, or feeding animals. All these activities were my first body movements. It was my first education. (Ibid.)

This view of dance as embedded in social practice and acquired from an early age also has, in both Laurence's and Ziya's accounts, a privileged place. It is significant in discussing dance and gender. When asked whether he had been aware of any suggestion that dancing was something that a man should not do, Laurence responded:

> No, I guess it was a very, the atmosphere was very healthy then. I think that there are, there have been other times, later times, when it was rarer and, a more extraordinary thing, but I don't think that anybody nowadays can really conceive just how much, for instance, dance we saw on film. And we went to the pictures every Saturday, you know. (Gard, 2006:123)

According to Gard, by merging these two narratives, a 'small but supportive town' and 'dance embedded in social practice', Laurence constructs a narrative which is at odds with much of the theoretical literature on male dancing. Gard further explains that it is generally argued that 'attitudes towards male dancing became more rather than less "healthy" to use Laurence's phrase' (ibid.:123). Gard thus points to the fact that theoretical literature suggests that the attitudes towards male dancers became 'softer' and more permissive over time. Laurence's case, like Ziya's, seems to argue quite the opposite: marking dance as a social phenomenon, embedded in everyday, 'normal' life. Despite similarities in their narratives, however, we must address Ziya's social and cultural background more carefully. Ziya did get into conflict with his father after finishing university (gaining a degree in mountain mining engineering) and deciding to embark on a career as a dancer. This resulted in his father refusing to talk to him for several years. He insists, however, that his father's objections were purely 'existential': he objected to his dance career only in comparison with a 'more prominent', 'respectable', and 'money making' engineering career. Ziya himself was quite taken aback when I suggested his father's objections might be connected to the ambiguities of the dance profession in terms of male sexuality:

> I don't think that my father was ... I think you should ask him. ... But his fear was not that I would became gay but his fear was an existential problem: 'I sent you to study and you became a dancer ... what is dance ... stupid thing ... there is no money from it ... finish your study and become an engineer. I spent all my life working so that you could become an engineer. I spent all my power to make you "my son the engineer"'. I think he was thinking that way. Perhaps he was thinking too: what does it mean to dance? But I don't think he was so imaginative to fear that I would become a gay. ... Maybe he was sometimes, I don't know, but we never talk about it. I am almost sure that for him the problem was existential. (Azazi, 2008a)

Ziya even noted that his father is nowadays proud of his son's career success. At first glance, this is at odds with the theoretical literature on dance and gender but also on gender and the Middle East (see Bodman and Tohidi, 1998). As the only son in an uneducated, poor, Muslim family, one would perhaps expect more disapproval and considerable pressure on Ziya, especially in terms of gender. Of course, the pressure to take a more 'respectable' career so that one day 'he could provide for his future family' (Azazi, 2008a) is an expectation based on gender roles. But nowhere in these accounts is dance seen as threatening to male sexuality. We may place this against the background of the gendered organization of both social and theatrical dance forms during the Ottoman era of Turkish history. In the Ottoman gender-segregated society, respectable Muslim women were not allowed to dance in public. Dancing was the preserve of Christian and Gypsy women (who were less socially respectable anyway) and of men (Kurt, 2008; see also Öztürkmen, 2003). For that reason men were more present in folk and social dances in the Ottoman Empire and, in fact, acclaimed twentieth-century French choreographer Maurice Béjart is ready to claim, on a similar basis, that dance is a 'man's affair':

> As for my celebrating the male dancer rather than the female dancer, I do this because I have come to realise that our first dancing was folk dancing, where the real dancers were always the males—they were the more important element of the dance. In early folk dancing, the women were merely beautiful—they followed, they helped. I mean look at Russian folk dancing. The men dance, and the women go around with handkerchiefs. In Japanese dancing, it's always the man. The same in African dancing. In Africa, women are often not allowed to dance or even

appear. Look at the American Indian dances. They were and are always executed by the males. And so, I found out that the origin of dancing was built on the power of the man. Women came to add beauty and femininity. (Gruen, 1975, cited in Gard, 2006:64; for similar claim see also Nikolais, 1966)

Although the dance profession has an extremely low place in the professional hierarchy in Turkey (Potuoğlu-Cook, 2006) it seems that there is no straightforward connection between dance and homosexuality. In societies where it is men who dance on almost every occasion, that assumption is, understandably, unsustainable, but the fact is that dance generally is not regarded as a respectable profession for either men or women (ibid.), and respect is reserved only for the successful few. For the tailor from Antakya, to have a son who is a professional engineer is certainly perceived as an upward move in terms of class mobility. The issue is more debatable with dance. However, Ziya's account suggests more subtle ways in which gender and class are intertwined. Ziya's first professional dance group, 'The Turquoise', formed in Istanbul, consisted of both male and female dancers. When asked to reflect on gender relations within the group in terms of who had 'leadership', Ziya responded that the 'ladies' definitely possessed the authority because they were from Istanbul, whereas the 'boys' were from Anatolia. This is, of course, much in the line with Ziya's 'boy from the village narrative'. On another occasion, when I interviewed a Turkish dancer and choreographer 'Samir', Ziya's friend and former member of 'The Turquoise', a similar pattern emerged. Both 'Samir' and Ziya (who was present during the interview) mark their passion for dance as a rural trait. They were 'boys from the streets' (Azazi,

2009), as opposed to educated and refined Istanbulites, and as such their desire to 'make it' in dance (and in the big city, I would add) led them to success ('Samir' is one of the most successful choreographers in Turkey).

However, Ziya's comment on the gender leadership within 'The Turquoise' is indicative of the way Turkish modernist development articulated gender and class. Kagitcibasi (1986) suggests that the status of women in Turkey greatly depends on an urban/rural divide, whereby women with urban employment and lifestyles enjoy far greater status than uneducated, rural women. The greatest divide is thus not solely across gender lines, but between urban and rural, or what is often referred to as modern and premodern. This could, at least partly, explain why Istanbul-born women could attain positions of leadership vis-à-vis their male colleagues from Anatolia: however it is worth remembering that the 'boys from Anatolia' gained success as solo dancers on the Istanbul dance scene.

So Ziya makes quite straightforward narrative connections between his childhood and his subsequent dance skills. His early years as a 'boy from the village' were marked by physical activities that paved his way to an interest in gymnastics during his university years, and later to dance. He remembers how he easily got good marks for physical classes at the university because he was a 'boy from the village'—it was easy for him. However there is more to his accounts on his childhood than just plain physical activity. He recalls how he had different interests in physicality from his male friends:

> Dunja: Did you experience pressure from your male friends to be 'more masculine'?

Z: I did, I did, but it was not my power and not my interest. For example, when we went to swim I wasn't the best swimmer or the most powerful to stay under water for longer. I was just enjoying being in the water and climbing in the rocks and jumping in a different ways ... so ... a kind of something extraordinary was my interest. Of course this was not my purpose, I was doing it intuitively. (Azazi, 2008a)

So, being interested in dance originated from something more ('extraordinary') than simple physicality. Although the precise knowledge about dance and specific skills did come much later, his early years are essential to his skill. Ziya's narrative about his childhood and his subsequent career choice indicates that his social upbringing was most important not only because of his physical abilities, which made him a technically good dancer, but also on account of his desire, which he connects with the purity and modesty of his rural upbringing. This made him, he recounts, determined and disciplined in pursuing his career. However, the importance of his childhood and the social environment in which he grew up resurfaces as an important factor in various stages of his dance career. When it comes to his dance aesthetic, especially Sufi dancing, the importance of dance in the social poetics of his early years will emerge again as constitutive to understanding Ziya's career choices and trajectories.

4. Doing Dance in Postsocialism: 'Alexander', 'Peter', and Igor

Like most of the dancers that Gard interviewed, none of the dancers I worked with had any 'life changing', 'revealing moments' when they decided to become dancers. Most of them, however, had a moment like that when they embraced a certain dance aesthetic or dance style. Where dance as a profession is concerned, it became an option emerging from different historical, social, and personal circumstances. The example of Romanian dancer 'Peter' is unique among the dancers I interviewed because he was the only one who had professional ballet training from an early age. In that sense, for him, as Gard noted for some of his dancers, 'becoming a dancer is a story without a beginning' (Gard, 2006:135). It is difficult to mark this as a life-changing moment, since at that age (ten years old), it is rather questionable whether we can speak of a decision making process. 'Peter' recalled being attracted to gymnastics, but he cannot recall his first memory of seeing dance:

> For me it was not about dance, but the body in some kind of ... it is the image of the gymnast that I remember. Even now when I watch gymnastics on the TV I remember that years ago I was trying to imitate that and to move on the music from the set. This stays with me quite strongly. ('Peter', 2008)

After noticing 'Peter's' interest in physicality, his parents enrolled him in dance classes held by a sports teacher. Soon however, at the age of ten, 'Peter' was admitted to a ballet school:

> During the communist regime there was always, once a year, some kind of scouting for talents. They were scouting for gymnasts and also for ballet dancers. They were just going to the cities and putting up posters for auditions for the ballet school. And my teacher, who was giving classes for kids, asked me if I wanted to go to this audition because I was the only boy in the class, and I moved well. Dunja: So, they were scouting for boys only?

> P: Not only for boys. Boys and girls. Of course boys were more rare ... As I lived next to the big city, my teacher asked my parents if it would be possible for me to go to this pre-selection in Braşov. So, I went there and I was pre-selected for the final audition in September in the city of Cluj-Napoca. ('Peter', 2008)

Thus, at the age of ten, 'Peter' moved to another town to train professionally. Soon however, because he was missing his family, he returned home, only to be readmitted to ballet school in Bucharest at the age of fifteen. Being in ballet professionally from that early age, he could not remember what exactly attracted him to it:

> Dunja: Do you remember why you wanted to be a dancer?
> P: I don't think that at that time I really understood what it meant to be a dancer. I wanted just to move, to jump, to do rolls on the floor ... It was not very clear to me even when I went to a ballet school, what dancing was all about. You are very young, you are still in childhood at that time and then suddenly you are in this school where you have these classes, and these teachers who do all these classical exercises, very physical, very difficult, very different from the normal ways of using the body ... And of course it was not easy for me. For the first time I was living outside my home, my hometown. ('Peter', 2008)

The practice of scouting for dancers could be seen as a way of institutionalizing male dancing from an early age that surely produces certain perspectives on gender and male theatrical dancing. Unlike Gard's dancers, who were ignored or who were given tennis rackets by parents when expressing an interest in dance in childhood, 'Peter's' parents willingly took him to dance classes when noticing his interest in moving. 'Peter's' own recollection that he initially connected his interests in movement with gymnastics may illuminate the situation. In socialist countries sport, ballet, and folk dance companies were encouraged and controlled by the state. Commenting on the interrelation between sport and politics in the USSR, Howell explains how 'sport and physical education [were] seen as helping to strengthen the health of the masses and aiding in the moral, intellectual and aesthetic development of the individual' (Howell, 1975:128). Moreover, sport and artistic success was used as a discrete field in the 'cultural wars' of the Cold War period (Prevots 1998; Cohen, 1987), and socialist states were putting considerable efforts into promoting sport and improving the quality of their sportsmen. As Anthony Shay observed: 'The U.S.S.R. utilized the technical prowess of dancers and athletes ... to suggest the power of a state capable of producing powerful world-famous performances' (Shay, 1999:39).

It is thus not surprising that, as a child, 'Peter' was much impressed by the image of the gymnast he saw on the television and that Romania ran state-organized mass talent searches. Ballet can be seen as a matter of prestige in this competitive area as well, and here we may recall the success of the Bolshoi Ballet, which reflected the very idea of the Soviet nation and, as such, became 'the perfect instrument for cultural diplomacy in the 1950s and later' (Nicholas, 2001:97). Soviet ballet underwent a massive change from the Ballets Russes that was well known on the Western stage. Compared with the emphasis on the artistic genius of Vaslav Nijinsky, new Soviet male dancers acquired different qualities: 'Words like "virile" and "masculine" were used frequently, the strength of partnering and vigour of attack often contrasted with British male dancing' (ibid.:87). Nicholas explains this change to the acrobatic in Russian ballet as a result of the deliberate injection of proletarian physical culture into the aristocratic ballet technique. It is worth noting that the same qualities of strength and acrobatic virility were demanded from female dancers as well. Ballet, as a profession of strong and dedicated men and women, was thus cleansed from its connection to femininity and it became a respectable profession for men. Furthermore, success in these endeavours could increase the status of individuals and their families, resulting in financial and career rewards as well as bolstering the nation's image. Even so, 'Peter' indicated that ballet remained less prestigious in the hierarchy of professional activities:

> Well … dance was, at that time, and of course I had discussions in my family … Can a boy become a dancer? Is this a proper job for a boy? But my mother supported me saying 'why not, if he likes to dance, if he wants to move.' So, somehow, my parents supported me in this journey I have had until now. If my parents hadn't been that open, I would not be here now. So I think that my family was an important factor in me becoming a dancer. ('Peter', 2008)

Although at this instance it is not clear why dance could not be seen as a 'proper' profession for a man, 'Peter' returns to the matter when recalling reactions of his male friends to his decision to go to Bucharest to train professionally:

> I had close friends, I don't know, people were not looking at me like this was something normal, when I said that I was going to Bucharest to become a dancer … They were asking me if I was sure in my decision. Was that how I want to spend my life? Usually it was about that this was not a proper job for a man, like … how are you going to support your family?
> Dunja: What about your parents?

> P: It was also their reaction. The surroundings were ... mmm ... basically it was not regarded as a proper job for man, it was not a very serious job. Serious is to be a doctor, lawyer, engineer. (Ibid.)

Similar to Ziya, the concern was expressed in existential rather than sexual terms, even among his friends. However, there were other remarks on gender and dance which mirrored those offered in Gard's research on dance, masculinity, and sexuality (see also Burt, 1995; Thomas, 2003). When discussing the actors on the Romanian dance scene, 'Peter' remarked how interesting it was to note that almost all of them were male, and he explained this by claiming that Romania is still a macho country and that the voices of female choreographers are not very strong. This reminds us of how gender inequality works in favour of men even if we talk about theatrical dance and its stigma of homosexuality.

In my research, Igor Koruga, from Serbia, was the first dancer who introduced a notion of gender and 'queer sensibilities' as somehow decisive for his experience of childhood and correspondingly for his artistic practice although he seems to distinguish between 'queer sensibility' and sexuality as such. In an interview where he talked about his upbringing and personal development he maintains that his upbringing was marked by his illness, about which more will be said soon, and a general feeling of being 'different' in an environment hostile to differences:

> I felt pressures all my life and somehow rejection because I was ... I don't know how to say this, it may sound like some sort of queer propaganda (laughter) ... In a sense it is really because I don't associate it with sexuality or sexual orientation ... I was born different because of my health

> and all that situation, and somehow my attitude towards reality and all that was happening was specific from the start because I had to take care of myself, to be always careful what I eat ... It complicated my relationship with my peers because I couldn't hang out with someone who is sick for example. In that sense I had to be careful, which, of course was very off-putting to other people and kids saw me as weird because of that. On the other hand I always carried a certain sophistication which didn't fit in those masculinity patterns which seems copied onto the boys in New Belgrade. (Koruga, 2013)

The story of his involvement in the performing arts started much later, but similar to Ziya, he maintains a narrative connection between his childhood and his dance practice. On many occasions during our series of interviews Igor emphasized the immense support he received from his family even when he had displayed interests 'unusual for boys' in an environment that would not encourage that kind of behaviour. Igor grew up in a working class, tough neighbourhood of New Belgrade and this is one of the cornerstories of his narrative. This is also an opening sentence of our first interview:

> I was born in Belgrade in 1985 and I spent my whole life here, more precisely at the New Belgrade because we weren't moving around as a family. My parents used to live in different part of the city but since I was born they remained settled and this is a context in which I grew up. I feel this is important, although I realized this only later, when I was in my twenties and when, during my university years, I started to hang out with people from different parts of the city. I realized how big difference is between say people who grew up in the city centre and my own childhood in New Belgrade. I am not trying to pass

> judgement here, but really we were in the situations where we acted like a 'sky and earth', and I find that peculiar. Well New Belgrade really is a special place for growing up because it is working class neighbourhood and people from all over the country were migrating during the war and found themselves here. They were working class families with working class kids and it was always tough ... you could feel it. (Ibid.)

The immense support for Igor was his family, the immediate 'safe' surrounding in an otherwise complex environment. Talking about this support, Igor noted that the interesting fact about his upbringing was the fact that he grew up surrounded mostly by women, especially since his parents divorced when he was a teenager:

> I think that the important fact is that I spent those very important, formative years with my mother and grandmother so I was surrounded by women ... Also as a child I spent my childhood with different nannies that took care of me. Those were always young women with something specific about them who went through my childhood and who had a big influence on me. I think this is really important as it developed certain sophistication on my side and turning me towards more 'artistic' waters. Now, I don't want to claim that the influence of women is generally beneficial for the development of artistic sensibilities (laughs), but by being under this influence I was less likely to subscribe to some dominant masculinity patterns characteristic for this context and especially for the context of New Belgrade. (Ibid.)

Unlike Ziya and 'Peter', Igor does not recall any straightforward interest in physicality. His narrative emphasizes experiences of creativity and tolerance towards differences which he connects with his parents and his home environment. Rather than being interested in physical experiences, Igor displayed an interest in entertainment, creativity and, very unlike Ziya and 'Peter', in a 'performing atmosphere' or even dramaturgy. Note here his first memories on dancing/performing:

> When I started dancing I was nineteen, twenty years, but I was sort of doing it much earlier. Let me remember, when I was seven, eight ... from my ninth year I was going to a music school, I played a violin and I've completed this lower music academy. But even before that, I formed with a friend (f) a theatre troupe with the children from my class, so we were making performances which we performed in nurseries where we had a deal ... we charged 50 para of one dinar a ticket and later we split that money amongst ourselves and bought ice-cream. However, it is precisely that 'economic' component complicated relationships in the troupe, because it was hard to split the money (laughs), so the troupe seized to exist. But it was great while it lasted, we made performances based on fairy tales and we have a few performances to perform several times. So now when I think about that it was truly great. Also we organized everything by ourselves, we went to those nurseries ourselves negotiated with the ladies who worked there and they were always happy to let us perform. We had rehearsals in our school. And of course there were always decisions to be made: who is going to be a prince, a princess ... I always had marginal roles but I was seriously involved in directing ... I guess that this is an aspect I have to this day. And then after this ... I don't know. I always liked to play with dolls and to make theatre performances with dolls, this may sound a bit pompous but even as a twelve-year-old I read Shakespeare and performed his plays with my dolls. (Ibid.)

The other very significant aspect of Igor's childhood and his life in general is his chronic illness. As a baby he was diagnosed with primary immunodeficiency, which is a type of bodily disorder when one's body does not produce enough antibodies to defend itself, so one is basically completely vulnerable to different types of diseases. Because of this, Igor has to receive therapy once a month and this profoundly affects different aspects of his life. To receive a therapy was not always so easy:

> I was diagnosed with this illness as a baby and the first five to six years were fine, my therapy was regular and I was healthy. However, at the beginning of the 1990s when the war broke there was a huge crisis. The therapy I was taking is imported from abroad and it's very expensive and because of the economic sanctions it wasn't possible any more to get it. So we had to figure out how ... and finally something was managed through the Red Cross. It was a very complex situation. As soon as I was diagnosed with this illness my mother became very active in preventing it. She became one of the co-founders of the international association of patients with this illness and today she is one of the board members. From the very beginning she was very active and she started travelling abroad and she attended seminars with other patients and doctors to learn how to cope with it or even how to fight it. So she was very active with other parents of the ill children to provide for therapy and she founded this organization. We were faced with an indifference and hostility of the state medical institutions, there was no money, it was crisis and war ... and then after the war we still have problems because the therapy is so expensive. And this fight lasts for twenty-five years, and every month it's the same question whether we will get our therapy or not. Officially, our national health care has to provide this for us, but every

> time government changes it's the same question and same fight all over again ... So during the war, when I wasn't receiving therapy, I had some health issues which made my life very complicated and made my childhood very different. In this sense also, I wasn't growing up as an ordinary child. I was sick a lot, absent from school, shielded from other children. And in this sense, my situation is also quite specific. (Koruga, 2013)

During my interviews with Igor we often ended up talking about his experiences connected with his growing up in New Belgrade and the general experience of war and desperation in the country. His first experiences with theatre were also somehow convened by the war:

> When she saw how I loved theatre, my mother had an idea to enrol me in some courses in the Centre for culture 'Old City' which was led back then by Ljubica Ristić Beljanski and which had a lot of drama based programs for children. However, those drama courses were not inspired only with more conventional drama curriculum but in that time, it was 1998, that centre is even today associated with some relevant contemporary dance troupes such as Mimart, Ergstatus, Swan teatar. All these troupes back then were all part of that ... well general initiative to come to terms with a difficult societal reality through art engagement. All the workshops were designed in that sense. I was in a group called 'coming-of-age theatre' and we were engaged in different projects. So, for instance, during the bombing in 1999 we had a project entirely designed to face this predicament and back then it was part of wider project called 'play against the violence' which was sponsored by the European Cultural Foundation. So from the very beginning I was involved with more alternative performing art scene in Serbia. (Koruga, 2013)

I wish to add here that Igor was most directly involved in the types of cultural policies employed by Europe to its 'immediate outside' exemplified by Vujanović's writings. The fourth dancer, Macedonian 'Alexander', does emphasize the importance of physicality. He was the only one of the dancers I worked with who was actively engaged in sport from an early age:

> I trained in athletics. I was good at it, people used to tell me that I had a strong character. And when I decide to do something I do it, and I see no obstacles. I started training because I was slightly overweight and my parents suggested I should lose some weight. During the training, I realized how body functions in space, how you develop speed, how to save breath because I trained long distance running ... And I learned to save energy for later, not to spend it all at once, and that helped me a lot. ('Alexander', 2008)

The relationship that male dancers have with sport, as a field of the 'appropriate' display of male bodies to spectatorship, was crucial to Gard's research: this is, according to him, the factor that can define what 'kind' of dancer each man is. In short, the relationship with sport reflects two opposite poles of male dancing: athleticism and physicality against expressiveness and emotionality. To a degree, all Gard's dancers claimed that dance is 'something more' than sport although it also relies on physicality. A number of Gard's dancers developed extremely negative views of sport as too competitive—especially the ones that suffered from their peers for not being very good at sport (and being interested in dance). Some were good at it but initially uninterested in sport. There is the interesting case of Ralph, a contemporary dancer, who used his sporting success as an 'excuse' to do dance classes: he lied to his peers and told them he was taking dance classes to improve his surfing coordination and balance, just to avoid bullying. In reality, it was vice versa.

Ziya, although occasionally playing football or basketball with his friends, did not develop any interest in sport, nor did he suffer because of that. He was, however, an exceptionally good gymnast during his university years. Igor almost never played any sport, but he was skipping the rope with his girlfriends. He remembered how he despised football; he didn't want to play basketball because he was afraid to hurt his fingers because of his violin playing; he didn't want to run. He mockingly noted how he was truly this 'artistic' soul who plays a violin and likes theatre. 'Peter's' case is exceptional since he started his professional ballet training at an early age. Trained as a ballet dancer, 'Peter' developed his career in contemporary dance, gradually developing negative attitudes towards ballet. At first, he distinguished ballet from sport much as Gard's dancers did, by equating the latter with a crude 'stupid' body and ballet, and dance in general, with an emotional, communicative body capable of conveying messages from the 'inside'. Later on, he admitted that he stopped making connections between ballet and dance and started connecting ballet with sport. He regards ballet purely as a form of physical training and technique that does not see dance practice as in any way linked to an 'inner self' or creativity. He also considers it a very competitive discipline, almost like sport, which can be connected with some negative experiences he suffered when living with other dancers in a student dormitory. He explains:

> Well ... I think that these memories I have about this period were like this because in Cluj it was very difficult,

> because we were small kids and the big ones made us wash their dirty clothing. We were rather like slaves for big children. It was normal. Also in Bucharest small kids had to do small, dirty things for the older ones. These were the rules. As you grow up, you have some privileges and with the years you sleep with less people in the room, you can sleep until late ... it was kind of a developing situation. ('Peter', 2008)

The atmosphere in these dormitories much resembled military training with the ritual humiliation of the newcomers, and we cannot trace any 'emotional geniality' of the ballet dancer in these accounts.

'Alexander' was the only one to gain a concrete, positive experience from sport and to make it relevant for his dance practice. 'The magic of theatre' is what attracted him to theatrical dance. When asked to recall his first memories of dance, 'Alexander' explained:

> My aunt works as an actress in the theatre and she used to take me there when I was a young boy. So, already when I was two or three years old, I was included as an extra in some performances for children. That love has stayed with me. ('Alexander', 2008)

Indeed, although he started dancing by copying MTV stars (Michael Jackson, for example), his 'true' understanding of dance as an art form comes from his exposure to and love of theatre. He recalls how he would always stay after performances when visiting companies performed in his town:

> There is a magic created whenever I enter [the theatre] to see a performance, which for me never ends with the applause of the audience. I used to stay longer in the

theatre every time or I would go backstage to see what was happening, what the set looked like and where everybody went when a performance ended. I wanted to know if the performance really ends when the audience exit, or if it ends when the audience leave and that's it ... I was interested precisely in that. ('Alexander', 2008)

'Alexander' also has a music degree and plays harmonica, which, we shall learn later, is also important in understanding his performing arts aesthetic. He also draws on the support that he gains from his parents, although he is the only dancer I worked with who had actually experienced being labelled homosexual because of his profession:

> Dunja: Why do you think there are fewer men in dance than women?
>
> A: Well in our country, and everywhere .. mmm ... When I started this kind of dancing I heard that there was a rumour circulating in town that I was homosexual. I decided to let people talk whatever they want, and I will do whatever I want ... And why? I think that they don't have self-respect and they don't believe in themselves but [they] easily get involved in some manipulations by their social surroundings, and they think they cannot make a mistake if they follow the majority.
>
> D: Is Prilep really such a small town that any rumour can easily circulate?
>
> A: Oh yes (he laughs), two hours is all that is needed for any story to be known. ('Alexander', 2008)

However, as I mentioned earlier on, 'Alexander' did not seem to be particularly bothered with this small-town feeling, since he still works and lives in Prilep. The level of disapproval may not be that pressing.

5. Concluding Remarks

The question, however, remains: To start with, how can one account for differences in the connection between dance and homosexuality in the narratives of the dancers I worked with and those in Gard's research? Although revealing different aspects of gender inequality in the dance profession, none of the accounts I collected presuppose a direct naturalized connection between homosexuality and theatrical dance. Further, my research findings on masculinity in the South East Europe and the Middle East do not correspond to the much established writing about gender relations in these areas, especially in terms of masculinities. In these concluding remarks I begin with addressing the issue of homosexuality and theatrical dance in these geopolitical areas, and then I briefly turn to the broader question of masculinity and gender.

With regard to the first point, as I have already indicated, throughout the Middle East, the Mediterranean and the South East Europe (Cowan, 1990; Kurt, 2008; Malefyt, 1998), it was historically men who enjoyed various forms of folk and social dancing while women were, to a degree, excluded. This does not mean that women were not dancing at all, but that they were facing more constraints over the occasions when they were 'allowed' to dance. Women usually danced in secluded, private spaces or at least under rather strict rules, as shown in research on Northern Greece (Cowan, 1990), and the Middle East (Shay and Sellers-Young, 2005; Potuoğlu-Cook, 2006). Also recall Béjart's observations that they were usually merely a modest accompaniment to men (see Gard, 2006:64). It is not only the region that is relevant here, for socialist states attributed great significance to folk dances. Shay notes how professional state-sponsored dance companies were crucial symbols of state power, so that for example even a 'small nation like Bulgaria had seventeen professional folk song and dance ensembles by the 1980s' (Ilieva 1994, cited in Shay, 1999:29). Thus, when the dancers I interviewed stated that there were 'no dance schools' when they were young, they do not count folk dancing, since almost every town in the former Yugoslavia, and I suspect in Romania too, had at least an amateur folk dance society (Opetchevska-Tatarchevska, 2009). The emphasis on the professionalization of folk dance created a distinct image of the male folk dancer as a strong, powerful, and dedicated athlete. Shay (1999) indicates that the images of female dancers were similar, noting the striking absence of any sensuality and sexuality in the dances of the celebrated Moiseyev Dance Company from the Soviet Union. Gender differences and sexual tensions were muted in favour of 'doll-like, forever smiling, happy individuals' (Shay, 1999:38). Shay believes that the absence of explicit gender representation in these dances is part of socialist ideological mechanisms that attempted to mask real gender asymmetries in society at large. This might be the case, but it is worth remembering that socialist countries did have strong politics of gender equality. As Gal and Kligman (2000) observe:

> The ideological and social structural arrangements of state socialism produced a markedly different relation between the state, men, and women than commonly found, for instance, in classic liberal parliamentary systems or in various kinds of welfare states. Gender as an organizing principle, male dominance, and gender inequality can be found in all these systems, but with profoundly different configurations. (Gal and Kligman, 2000:5)

Another possible reason for the apparent disconnection between male theatrical dance and homosexuality in the accounts of the dancers that I researched may lie in the fact that secular theatrical dance, both ballet and modern dance, is historically a strictly Western European and American invention (Russia being an exception). Turkey and South East Europe simply lack this internal context of an early bourgeois development when the explicit and implicit connections between dance and the 'effeminate' were made. Thus, it was during socialism in South East Europe and modernization in Turkey, with its special agendas on gender and professional dancing, that theatrical dance and professional folk dance brought certain kinds of male and female with strong, athletic bodies on the stage and marked dance as a respectable profession for men.

Further, the masculinities I encountered in the narratives of the dancers I researched are at odds with the literature on gender and South East Europe. Firstly, we have seen that the anxieties connected to dance as a profession for men, were often formulated as existential rather than sexual. Of course the pressure on men to have 'more respectable careers' in order to be providers for a family is an expectation based on the male gender role. But masculinity is here defined in material terms—a 'good man' is one who can materially provide for his family. In the narratives of the dancers that Gard researched we encounter no hints at all of any professional hierarchization in this sense—being a man is defined in strictly sexual terms. Of course, this was Gard's research agenda, but so was mine, with profoundly different outcomes as this chapter has shown. Further, regarding the economic aspects of the dance profession in his research, Gard himself states that stories of economic hardships 'do not figure prominently' (Gard, 2006:168) in the accounts of the dancers he interviewed. Secondly, much recent literature on gender and the South East Europe is preoccupied with the postsocialist period when, due to the economic transition (Einhorn, 1993; Rueschemeyer, 1998; Gal and Kligman, 2000; Jaffe Robbins, 1994) and the wars in the former Yugoslavia (see Ramet, 1999; Jovanović and Naumović, 2001), gender relations and equality are deemed to have deteriorated significantly. It seems that there is no satisfying dialogue or any kind of consensus between Western and Eastern European gender scholars as to how to theorize gender relations during real socialism (see Einhorn, 1993; Keough, 2006; Simpson, 2004). The literature on gender issues in postsocialist Europe as well as in the Middle East has paid far more attention to femininity than to masculinity, which is perhaps understandable, given that the academic field of gender studies started as a feminist project for fighting gender inequality.

Therefore, it seems to me that the narratives of the male dancers I worked with, especially when recounting their first interest in dance, give us an interesting perspective—a glimpse into worlds that remained, to a degree, unknown due to the lack of academic attention. These narratives reveal different parameters of thinking about masculinity and gender relations in general. In the case of Ziya Azazi we have seen that the narrative of 'a village boy that wants to make it in the big city' figures greatly in both his and his father's concerns. Here, the urban-rural divide cuts across the gender divide. For those of us dancers that grew up during socialism, we experienced personal and subtle dealings with state-proclaimed gender equality and prevailing male dominance in these societies. This relationship created different, even if contradictory, masculine identities. Again, I am not claiming that socialism easily produced a gender equal society in which men and women could choose whatever profession they liked without any pressures. However, it is local details we are looking for, the small narratives of everyday life that reveal its complexities and intervene in a global theory of masculinity and femininity.

Colour Plates

Plate 1: Ziya Azazi in *Dervish* by Kerem Sanliman (Istanbul, 2008).

Plate 2: Ziya Azazi in *Dervish* by Kerem Sanliman (Istanbul, 2008).

Colour Plates

Plates 3 and 4: Ziya Azazi in *Dervish* by Kerem Sanliman (Istanbul, 2008); and Ziya Azazi with the author in Budapest in 2008.

Plates 5 and 6: Igor Koruga in *Come Quickly, My Happiness is at Stake* (2012); and in *Temporaris*, a co-authored performance (2011-13).

Colour Plates

Plate 7: Igor Koruga in *The Scale* (2011) with Josephine Larson Olin.

CHAPTER 4

DANCE PERFORMANCE AS LABOUR AND PRODUCTION

1. Introduction

> I think what makes a big difference is that I'm an artist and as such I have different life than normal people. I mean, you work on Saturdays and Sundays, you work in many different spaces, you change many flats, always on the move ... Your personal life sometimes doesn't matter because you have to do the job. If you have a performance booked and if you don't feel well you have to do it because there are certain constraints that work on the market and certain rules that you have to play by. ('Peter', 2008)

> I've told you already how the situation is in the state of constant insecurity, an insecure life. Maybe it is important to note that whenever I talk to the people from different professions, they are always impressed, it all looks fascinating to them. They see you travel, you meet a lot of new people, you are conceptualizing the reality and so on. But in reality it's one hell of an exhaustive life. For me it is difficult because I find it tiresome to change bed every two-three weeks, to be in different place, in a different city, to constantly shift realities and contexts, to forget whom did I meet and when ... it all becomes mentally overbearing. And health-wise ... all that changing of climates and environments reflects badly on my health. Finally ... that sort of intensive life where everything is temporary and somehow blurry, well, we talked about this already. In fact, everything appears to be concrete and transparent but in reality everything is superficial ... as if ... I don't know ... it all extends across your private and professional lives. (Koruga, 2013)

Dance Performance as Production

There is an underlying assumption in the current debates on globalization and transnationality: it is the assumption that the immaterial and creative (artistic) work is central for understanding new flexible and mobile political, sexual, and national identities (Dirlik, 1998; Amoore, 2002; Head, 2003; Ducatel, Webster, and Hermann, 2000). 'Peter's' statement above, for instance, describes the way his life is constantly on the move (travelling, shifting, adapting) and the way the boundary between his private and professional life is blurred. This continuum between professional and private lives, and emphasis on flexibility and mobility in the emerging labour patterns figures significantly, not only in the sociological descriptions of the present of globalization (Castells, 1996), but they also reflect the forms of oppression and modes of dominance in post-Fordist capitalism (Hardt and Negri, 2000). Therefore, this chapter is going to look at the professional life of a contemporary dancer as it collides with his/her private life. In doing so, the chapter will discuss several interrelated issues around artistic labour. Firstly, the chapter will discuss the political implications of dance as immaterial labour in the context of South East Europe, referring to the globalization theory of Michael Hardt and Antonio Negri. Secondly, it will analyze dance as a production process, drawing on Marx's idea of production as a totality of social relations and its implications for the contemporary condition of capitalism. This will involve a move from a discussion of immaterial labour to one of the creative industries and of the distinction between 'creative' and 'non-creative' work through the examination of the notion of dance technique in the narratives of my dancers. Following Hamera (2007), the chapter will treat dance technique as deeply political—not simply 'strategy for moving', but 'series of tactics for living'. Dance technique negotiates gender representations and resistances, the relationship between art and life, and issues of discipline and authority (ibid.:61). Finally, the chapter will question the notion of artistic labour in general giving a few concluding points on changing modes on labour in globalization.

2. Immaterial Labour and Dance in South East Europe

Michael Hardt and Antonio Negri's Empire presents a grand and unified vision of the world in which old forms of imperial modernity are no longer effective and which testifies to the rise of a new form of global sovereignty. As already explained, they argue that Empire constitutes a borderless world which effectively creates and recreates borders anew. It is a form of capitalism which relies on communicative, creative, and affective work, i.e. 'immaterial work', meaning that for a number of professional tasks the process of creating is internal to the product itself. Hardt and Negri maintain that immaterial labour has become a prototype of all labour and it is on the basis of this immaterial work that the new subjects of Empire develop a particular emancipatory politics. These subjects make up 'the multitude', the 'living alternative that grows within Empire' (2004:xiii). Hardt and Negri argue that this new political subject of resistance should replace previous notions of social subjects such as people, masses, and the working class, all of which were based on exclusion. In contrast, they claim, the multitude as a political subject is based on multiplicity, difference and inclusion. Therefore,

> The multiplicity is composed of innumerable internal differences that can never be reduced to unity or a single identity—different cultures, races, ethnicities,

gender and sexual orientation; different forms of labor; different ways of living; different views of the world; and different desires … Thus the challenge posed by the concept of multitude is for social multiplicity to manage to communicate on and act in common while remaining internally different. (Ibid.:xiv)

Thus, for Hardt and Negri the hegemonic and dominant productive force within Empire is precisely immaterial labour created by circuits of collaboration and cooperation (networks) which are maintained across the globe, and which, in terms of revolutionary potential have supplanted industrial labour. In the terms proposed by Hardt and Negri, South East European dance artists, as immaterial labourers, could be said to be engaged in such processes of collaboration and cooperation. They are therefore directly included in producing not only the reality of the South East Europe and the EU, here and there, but also in the production of social forms of life, i.e. the biopolitical. The differences between them, according to Hardt and Negri's framework, are not obstacles in the creation of political subjects ('the multitude') as the critics would have it, but actually their great advantage and challenge at the same time.

The challenge is, indeed, formidable. How are differences without politically recognized similarities supposed to form a common field of resistance? The main argument of Hardt and Negri is that immaterial labour directly produces forms of life – i.e. it is biopolitical, since the regulation of social space and social relations is what it does. Thus, in principle, immaterial labourers have direct access to regulating all forms of social life (there are no owners since the production is directly social) and they are therefore able to create a democracy from below without any formal representatives.

The multitude as a new concept of political subjectivity has faced many criticisms. At best, it has been argued, it remains 'a hypothesis', 'a wishful thinking', and open field of investigation, but it does not exist yet (Lotringer, 2003:15). In addition, Lotringer characterizes immaterial workers as:

> mobile and detached, adaptable, curious, opportunistic and cynical, also toward institutions; they are inventive and share knowledge through communication and language; they are mostly depoliticized and disobedient. (Lotringer, 2003:17)

So, the question is: how can one form a political subject out of this ambiguous assemblage of differences? Žižek (2004) questions the potential of the multitude as a site of resistance against Empire, asking how it functions, or more precisely:

> What a given field of multitude excludes, what it has to exclude to function. There is, hence, always a non-multiple excess over multitude. Take a multiculturalist identity politics. Yes, a thriving multitude of identities—religious, ethnic, sexual, cultural—asserted against spectre of antiquated 'class reductionism and essentialism'. However, it was noted long ago by many a perspicacious observer, in the mantra of 'class, gender, race', 'class' sticks out, never properly thematized. (Žižek, 2004:197)

Let us, however, engage with the potentialities of the term discussing them in the context of South East Europe and the new modes of labour in globalization. In this sense, I will focus here on the implications of Hardt and Negri's writing on the multitude and the particular and desired democracy outside the framework of the state that they envision. I will address precisely the implications of the 'global multitude' in societies 'still' bounded by the 'sedentary logic of the state' (D'Andrea, 2007).

To begin with, all of my interviewed dancers to a degree present paradigmatic examples of immaterial labour: it can be said that sharing knowledge and communication, creating networks, pursuing projects (Lotringer, 2005) is what my dancers live on. None of them has a permanent, fixed-salary job. For instance, the creation of the 'Balkan Dance Platform' festival, the first festival that showcases performance work from South East Europe, was 'Peter's' personal initiative following a chat on a coffee break with the Bulgarian dancer and cultural manager Dessi Gavrilova. All these dancers are also very mobile, adaptable, curious, and very cynical towards institutions. They are also depoliticized in the sense that they are not active in the political life of their respective countries, through party membership or other state-related channels. Nevertheless, some of them, like Igor and 'Peter', would consider their work to be political, ideally making an impact on social space or aspiring to do so.

Having underlined similarities, it is important to stress differences as well. Ziya, for example, managed to have an international career because of his Austrian citizenship. In 2008, he reported how he had approximately seventy-two performances in different towns across the globe, which implies he was in a different place every fifth day of the year. The other three dancers, however, have had only relative mobility, at least until recently. Because of the changes in visa regimes for citizens of Romania, Serbia, and Macedonia, the mobility enjoyed by Ziya was simply out of the question for them. EU visas for Romania were lifted in January 2007, a year before I started my research with 'Peter'. Although he greatly enjoyed his newly acquired mobility, the major part of his dancing career was developed during an era of travelling restrictions. For Macedonia and Serbia, the EU Schengen visa regime was lifted on 19 December 2009, after the major part of my research with these dancers had been conducted. Generally, Igor, 'Alexander', and 'Peter' developed their careers in relation to the relative restrictions imposed by the EU on its 'immediate outside' (Jansen, 2009).

This situation also had another significant consequence for those South East European dancers: a close association with their respective 'nation-states', relative to that of Ziya Azazi, for example. One important argument of various globalization theories, including Hardt and Negri's, is that the political significance of nation-states has diminished dramatically. Hardt and Negri's immaterial workers are stateless beings inasmuch as Empire is the global formation of capital that does not recognize any formal boundaries. Yet I found that immaterial workers in South East Europe are in a slightly different position from immaterial workers with other, more favourable passports. The economies of the South East European states were not straightforwardly integrated into capitalist globalization during socialism, and the wars and social unrest made it fairly unattractive territory for foreign investment in the immediate postsocialist period. The position of the immaterial worker in postsocialist states carries, in fact, the signature of both the condition of immaterial labour (artists and intellectuals) during socialism (with a relatively strong relationship with the 'nation-state'), and of the immaterial worker of globalization (detached from the state and active in the NGO sector in a developing 'civil society'—the latter being especially important in the war-torn former Yugoslavia). This basically means that, despite working mainly in an NGO sector, their work is in close proximity to the state (at least in the case of 'Peter' and

Igor). In short, they do not call for the abandonment of the state altogether in favour of some kind of global democratic community, which is where Hardt and Negri locate the resistance of immaterial labour of the Empire. On the contrary, they envision a more global, democratic society, but through the means made available by the state. The state, for them, is responsible for providing its citizens with the right to mobility in a 'borderless world'. Usually, these views are aired as a criticism of state insufficiency and inability to come to terms with the new times[15] but nevertheless the state very much exists and is accorded utmost importance. In 'Peter's' narrative especially, the old socialist ways of doing things (in the arts for example) are criticized but in a manner that is still part of the socialist world view in which the state itself gives a platform for intellectuals to air their views. I will not dwell on this issue further, except to say that, perhaps, this is not a specifically postsocialist situation at all. Maybe Hardt and Negri's thesis on a stateless Empire is simply false, in that they neglect the role of territorially organized state power in the reproduction of capitalist social relations (see Mertes, 2003; Wood, 2003). The anthropologist Aihwa Ong rightfully stresses that 'Transnationality induced by accelerated flows of capital, people, cultures, and knowledge does not simply reduce state power, but also

---

[15] The focus here was often on the inability to get rid of some 'habits' inherited from socialism. This is especially present in 'Peter's' comments on the system of arts funding and the understanding of the arts in general. Interestingly, this criticism has a strong temporal dimension: governmental funding policies are seen as remnants from the past and not as the result of negotiating the present. South East Europe is recognizably represented as lagging behind the West.

stimulates a new, more flexible and complex relationship between capital and governments' (Ong, 1999:21). As it goes, the nation-state remains an essential instrument for global capital and therefore it is still a main zone of conflict.

Keeping in mind this discussion on the state, let me proceed with the question of immaterial labour. Overwhelmingly, the dancers I interviewed had extremely busy schedules and they barely found time to meet me for interviews. Many of our interviews started with talking about project deadlines, hard work and lack of time for anything. For this reason, some of the interviews were conducted on trains, for example. Project-based work means that sometimes these dancers do not know if they are going to be paid for it or not ('Peter', 2008). To Tsianos and Papadopoulos (2006) the expression 'I don't have the time', which I heard so many times during my research, is an explicit statement of the contemporary worker's subjectivity. This includes an embodied experience of restless movement across the continuous time of life, i.e. intermingling work and non-work, work and leisure time, etc. Thus Tsianos and Papadopoulos conclude that the expression '"I don't have the time" is the paradigmatic figure for the subjective internalization of non-disposal over one's own labour power' (ibid.:10). Tsianos and Papadopoulos draw on Marx's notion of labour power and alienation. For Marx too labour power is a function of time: what a worker 'sells' and what distinguishes him/her from the slave is his/her capacity to reproduce labour power for a limited amount of time. Novak, thus, concludes with Marx: 'The labourer is only "free" to become a commodity once the reproduction of his or her body becomes both a function of time and an embodiment of time—what Marx calls a quantity of "congealed labour time"' (Novak, 2007:137).

Dance Performance as Production

Thus, the dissolution of the distinction between work and non-work time is what renders problematic the new regime of work. Since the immaterial labourer cannot sell his/her labour power for any fixed time, in exchange for a fixed wage, he or she resembles the slave more than the worker. In this light we can see 'Peter's' almost virtual cultural organization whose existence depends on insecure funding which employs people and rents an office space just for the time being. When there is no money, the organization is 'Peter' himself with his computer in his home. Likewise Igor's constant anxiety about the number of projects he needs to juggle to survive and remain active in the two scenes: Berlin and Belgrade. Or take the account of the Serbian dancer, 'Ivan', stating that he is always on the verge of starvation, since his work is of the kind where he gets a fair amount of money per project, but then there are not enough projects to keep him going. A similar account was provided by Ziya: he believes he is fairly well paid per performance, but there is no money for the creation and rehearsal process at all. Apart from this, however, as I have already indicated, the South East European artist as an immaterial worker still stands in a peculiar relationship to the nation-state since, due to his or her lack of mobility, he or she still depends on its market and (limited) funding.

'Alexander's' case is slightly different from the other dancers. He is the only one who has a studio at his disposal as part of a deal with a state theatre in his town. In exchange for this privilege he is obliged to give free dance classes for high school pupils in Prilep. Thus, he has a secure rehearsal place necessary to pursue projects (for which he is getting paid) and to build his career, but he is not getting paid by the state for the classes. This is a peculiar intermingling of the state and stateless, corporate driven economy. The state cannot provide for its subjects in terms of job and salary, but it can provide certain means for these subjects to be more eligible in the economy of the other kind. In 'Alexander's' case, thus, the state is even more present as a silent partner in the other kind of economy. 'Alexander' also has a stronger national identity than the other dancers. By this I do not refer to an abstract idea of belonging to a nation, but to indicate that 'Alexander' relies on and works with the 'nation-state' on more personal and intimate levels. He reported an anecdote with the Macedonian Ministry of Culture when he applied for funding for the international Dance Web programme, held in Vienna. When he went to the Ministry, in person, and introduced himself to the ladies working there, they cried: 'But how come we don't know about you at all? You have to come and have coffee with us from time to time!' 'Alexander' laughingly responded: 'But if I am having coffee with you all the time, how would I find time to do anything else?' (meaning: if I were drinking coffee with you here (losing my time) then I would not be here asking for funding at all since I would not have time to do anything — to work). This anecdote sums it up nicely: 'Alexander' is directly interpellated by the state in order to get closer, by developing a more personal relationship with its bureaucrats (the ladies in the Ministry), but the point I wish to emphasize is that 'Alexander' already feels relaxed about going to the Ministry in person, that he is apparently close enough. There is less of a sense of the state being somewhere 'up' there, an abstract machine which is so frustrating to 'Peter' and Igor. But the other side of this anecdote is also telling: 'Alexander' does not have time, and if he made time for the coffee drinking ritual in the Ministry of Culture, he would not have time to work.[16]

3. Dance Performance as Production: From Marx to Virno

The concerns over the production and consumption of dance performances on the (art) market, as we have already seen, have increasingly come to represent a dominant production mode in 'new dance' practices identified by Lepecki. As this argument goes, if choreography as a product of dance is to survive it should be emancipated from its modern dance definitions based on the autonomy of the author. The 'new dance' practices thus operate to dismantle the stable notion of choreography and to problematize authorship 'even if such orientation mainly results in a new aesthetic ("new look") of research and small scale work' (Cvejić, 2007).

The concern over performance production and (as) product is not confined to dance scholarship. Peggy Phelan's seminal *Unmarked: The Politics of Performance* explicitly connects (theatrical) performance to unproductivity. Phelan celebrates the political potential of performance as a representation without reproduction that escapes the production cycle of capitalism. Her argument is that because performance vanishes precisely at the point of its production it disappears into the memory and into the realm of unconsciousness where it escapes regulation and control (it accesses the Lacanian Real). Because performance is consumed at the moment of production and does not make for a material commodity, Phelan claims that it clogs the

---

[16] 'Alexander' did get support from the Ministry of Culture on that and on many other occasions, despite not developing this coffee drinking ritual.

smooth machinery of capitalist production (1993:148). Here I will not develop an in-depth, critique of Phelan's argument (see Joseph, 2003), but I will point to the fact that it relies on a rather simplified interpretation of Marx's theory of production. To Marx, production is the totality of social relations in society. Marx thus explicitly states that production is not simply the reproduction of the physical existence of individuals but it is a definite form of expressing their life. Individuals express their life so they are individuals. Marx thus asserts that 'Men have history because they must *produce* their life, and because they must produce it in a *certain* way: this is determined by their physical organization; their consciousness is determined in the same way' (Marx, 1969, cited in Tucker, 1980:158, emphasis original). Hence, not only are individuals and social relations formed and expressed in production but they in turn make production possible.[17] In that sense, Phelan fails to account for the totality of social relations implied in the production (and consumption) of the performance.

In stark contrast to Phelan, Paolo Virno (2003) and Miranda Joseph (2003) claim that performance is precisely a kind of product in which the act of production is essential. Joseph even adds that 'it is clear that such vanishing products are precisely what contemporary capitalism thrives on' (2003:393). So, returning to the question of choreography, there is no opposition between choreography (product) and work-in-progress (non-product), but both are a kind of product to which the activity of producing is internal and essential. Both are the result of a certain kind of labour which Virno, following Marx, renders 'linguistic-virtuosic'

---

[17] I shall elaborate on this point later when addressing Marx's writings on embodiment and social relations.

and Hardt and Negri 'immaterial'.[18] Virno highlights the production of post-Fordist virtuosos, comparing it with the kind of production of Marx's 'unproductive' [19] labourers:

> While the virtuoso in the strictest sense of the word (the pianist, the dancer, for instance) makes use of a well-defined score, that is to say, of an end product in its most proper and restricted sense, the post-Fordist virtuosos, 'performing' their own linguistic faculties cannot take for granted a determined end product … virtuosity for the post-Fordist multitude is one and the same as virtuosity of the speaker: virtuosity without a script, or rather, based on the premise of a script that coincided with pure and simple dynamis, with pure and simple potential. (Virno, 2003:65)

Two significant implications emerge from this quote. Firstly, for Virno, a dancer undoubtedly produces end-products: a

---

[18] For detailed discussions on historical relations between the categories of 'performance' and 'labour' in Western critical thinking and Marxist theory in particular see BADco and de Campos (2012) and Wikström (2012).

[19] Although Marx almost never addressed art and immaterial work in his writings, except for some brief discussions on immaterial work (in the *Theories of Surplus Value*, for example) he renders this work 'unproductive'. In a footnote in *Grundrisse* Marx comments on the unproductiveness of immaterial (art) work through the distinction between the work of the piano maker and the pianist: 'The pianomaker produces capital; the pianist merely exchanges his labour for income. But the pianist produces music and satisfies our musical sense. In fact he does this: his work does produce something, but it is not therefore productive labour in the economic sense, any more than the work of a madman is productive when he produces hallucinations. Labour is only productive so long as it is producing its antithesis' (Marx, 1939, cited in McLellan, 1971:79).

choreography or a 'script'. Secondly, I have already indicated in Chapter Two that with the emergence of conceptual dance, dancers themselves became preoccupied with the dismantling of the notion of dance as a (market) product. In doing this, dance work moved towards the definition of immaterial labour, but it seems that there is no escape from the production/consumption circle.[20] In this sense, for our discussion about the political potential of performance, the formal should not take centre stage: it does not really matter whether we watch highly elaborate, virtuosic choreography or under-elaborated work-in-progress. What counts are always the social relations, life itself (Boltanski and Chiapello, 2005), produced and reproduced among dancers, dance institutions, and dance audiences in the very act of the dancer's labour. As Virno points out: '"When the product is inseparable from the act of producing", this calls into question the personhood of the one who performs to that of the one who has commissioned the work or for whom it is being done' (Virno, 2003:68).

Taking this into account, therefore, dance performance calls into question the totality of social relations involved in its production, since social relations are both conditioned by and originate from the division of labour. In a similar vein, Alice Rayner (2002) is looking at theatre 'work' in a Marxist sense as a totality of social relations involved in the production of a theatre piece. Rayner is interested in relationships between stage crew on the one hand, and

---

[20] In this vein, Lesage calls for the abandonment of the ontological distinction between immaterial labour and material labour which is, to him, nothing more than fruitless discussion. Instead he recognizes the 'general tendency of the becoming of the performative of labour' (2012:14).

actors/directors on the other, tracing the tensions inherent in theatre work. [21] To her, glossing over and hiding these tensions is, ideologically speaking, the system on which theatre 'works'. Addressing the actor/stage crew duality and work, Rayner asserts that:

> When a stage crew comes on during the intermission to change scenery or props in full view of the audience, it announces in effect, 'we are here and not here, doing real thing that you see ... We are working but we are not signifying'. 'Work' is marked as real, it is not signifying representational action and is rather, as Marx would have it, a productive act. (Rayner, 2002:537–8)

To Rayner it is precisely this gap between the 'real' work of a stage crew and the 'non-work' of actors and directors that is the crux of theatre 'magic'. To her, theatre practice reproduces a structure of desire, of the audience's desire to reveal more—'a desire for difference between imaginary and the real' (ibid.:539). This desire, according to her, can be seen as ideological in a Marxian sense—it is an ideology on which theatre 'works'.

Theatre and dance work, thus, has to be concealed in order for a certain 'illusion' to be put forward. Rayner claims that that illusion is fostered by the division between the 'work' of the technicians and the 'non-work' of actors and directors. She traces tensions embedded in this division, and, significantly for our discussion of immaterial labour, shows how these differences are experienced as a division between

---

[21] For a similar discussion referring to the work of a theatre crew and their relations with dancers and directors in the ballet world see Wulff (1998).

physical and mental labour, or, in Rayner's terms, between material and conceptual work:

> The actuality of the labourer creates its own affective sense of privilege for the technician and its own version of otherness, which for the technician often entails at a minimum an ironic view of performance, of actors and directors, of audiences and critics, and especially of academics. ... Unlike the wilful ignoring of the technical crew by audience and critics, the sense of ironic distance or contempt follows from the asymmetry of the relationship between the conceptual and the material practices. The asymmetrical exercise of power between the regulatory forces of the conceptual domain and material practices can produce an effective hostility in both. The hostility occurs not only because of a difference in power, however, but more fundamentally because of a difference in needs. The conceptual domain will always need material to realize its demands; it is dependent. (Ibid.:545)

Rayner's argument is worth quoting at length because it has peculiar implications for thinking about dancers' labour. We could trace this tension between conceptual dance and ballet (and to some extent modern dance), or between what Birringer (2005) terms 'Konzepttanz' and 'Tanztanz', or between dancers who work with ideas and concepts (even when those ideas include critical reflection on the embodied, material side of dance) and dancers who work exclusively with the body (even when that work includes a certain choreographical concept). Rayner identifies a certain tension if not hostility between those who work with the sweat of their bodies (technicians) and those who work with their brains (genius artists, actors, directors, and dancers). The paradox here is of course that actors and dancers also work predominantly with their bodies, since most performances still rely on the embodied presence of performers and audiences. Further to this, regardless of the conceptual turn, large numbers of dancers still work through the sweat of their bodies and view their profession as 'body work'. This question is especially significant concerning the fact that dance differs from other service, body-to-body labour, in that, at least for many ballet dancers, to describe their work is to use almost exclusively corporeal terms: pain, exhaustion, muscle strains, etc. (Wulff, 1998).

Further, as already indicated, dance studies scholars have on the whole been concerned with the issue of the representation of dancing bodies on the stage, without questioning the production process as such. In that sense dance studies assumed that while a dancer uses his/her body (or that a dancer is a body), this body somehow does not work, i.e. it does not produce. More interestingly, a significant proportion of dance scholarship, especially with the rise of postmodern dance as defined by Banes and postmodern and modern dance criticism, criticizes ballet on the grounds that its aesthetic of effortlessness and weightlessness oppresses the ballerinas' bodies (Summers-Bremner, 2000; Innes, 1988). As we have discussed already in Chapter One, Sally Banes claims that part of the postmodern rebellion in dance was directed at the inhuman treatment of dancers' bodies in pursuing spectacular virtuosity. Thus, in the spirit of democracy, postmodern dance included non-trained, non-perfect, non-dancing bodies in dance performance. However, in dance scholarship the discussion about non-trained bodies in dance performance and dance technique in general is rarely launched from the point of view of the dancer's labour (bodies that actively produce), but is rather concerned with the issue of power that regulates and normalizes the very notions of body and physicality (bodies that reflect;

bodies that resist). Perhaps the question of body and power has never been discussed in terms of labour because of the fact that postmodern theoretical aspirations regarded bodies as signifying machines, as texts, rather than as labouring machines (McNally, 2001). To McNally, much work grounded in postmodern theory, whether we term it poststructuralism or deconstruction, has banished the real human body—the biocultural, sensate, and labouring body—from the sphere of social life. That is why Banes's writing about non-dancing bodies in Rainer's project became a specifically postmodern dance manifesto, i.e. it concerned a specific aesthetic of post-modern dance, rather than an investigation of the corporeality of dance work.

Consequently, Alexandra Carter (2004b) claims that the notion of dance performance as a job is still unexplored in dance scholarship, implying that the research in dance should include the totality of relations that make for the dance work. Thus, she states:

> The glamour of the ballerina is fascinating, but also too is the question 'how much did she get paid?' We know about big names, and we will probably never know the actual small names, but we can be alert to the notion that the dance event is produced not only by individual creative artists but by unacknowledged armies of dancers, walk-ons, administrators, scene builders and movers, front-of house, publicity and marketing people and so on. (Carter, 2004b:16)

Therefore, it is perhaps necessary to reopen the question of the body once more but this time with a focus on dance as production and the dancing body as a working body. One possible way to do this is through a discussion of the tensions between ballet and contemporary dance techniques, since all the dancers I interviewed had quite elaborate and passionate views on the relationship between them. This in turn can be theoretically developed through a closer look at ballet technique and its implication for understanding the totality of dance labour in general.

4. Creative Work Against Body Work: Changing Economies of Dance Labour

I have already argued (see above), through Marx's writing on productive labour and the recent shift towards immaterial labour, that dance performance is a certain kind of product which, at the height of the 'century of the performance' (McKenzie, 2001) gained new momentum and significance in shaping the art world and world of commerce. Up to now we can conclude that dancers in general are immaterial workers whose product of labour is the very act of producing whatever the product is. Having this in mind, perhaps a more fruitful discussion of dance labour can be launched through the notion of the 'creative industries'. We have already seen how the notion of creativity shapes the 'new spirit of capitalism' (Boltanski and Chiapello, 2005) and through a brief discussion of dancer Xavier Le Roy in Chapter Two we saw how the opposing logics of art and commerce coexist embodied in the new figure of the 'creative worker'. According to Graham Murdock, cultural industries have gained particular significance at the centre of political debates about the transformation of contemporary capitalism (Murdock, 2002:15). My point here is that perhaps the difference between 'think' dancers and 'dance' dancers is best understood not through the opposition material/ immaterial labour but through the opposition between what came to be seen as creative versus non-creative work.

Conceptual dancers are creative workers, since their work-life corresponds to the new idea of work and the relation between work and life (leisure) in particular.

Bearing this in mind, I wish, however, to reopen the question of the body, dance technique, and virtuosity in dance with a special emphasis on ballet technique. It has already been a matter of discussion that the advancement of modern dance at the beginning of the twentieth century had been perceived as liberation of the (female) body (of the ballet dancer) from the rigorous and unnatural treatment of ballet technique. Under the growing influence of physical culture movements (Au, 2002; Howe, 1996; Franko, 1995), it was believed that the body should be returned to its natural flows, rhythm, and beauty because only that body was able to communicate universal meanings.

This 'war' against crude technique, pain, and 'cramped muscles' (Howe, 1996:12) did not stop here, however, and the second wave of the anti-technique movement came with American minimalist dance and Yvonne Rainer's 'No to Spectacle' (1979) manifesto during the 1960s and 1970s. While early modern dancers conveyed a criticism of ballet technique by offering an alternative body technique which was deemed more 'natural', Rainer's work is unique in that she offered an intellectual contemplation on immanent questions of dance.[22] As Banes claims:

> Some considered Rainer 'the dullest in [her] relenting defiance of everything conventional in theatre and dance,' charging that she offered nothing more than 'utter boredom' and 'non-dance'. But what Rainer offered, rather

---

[22] André Lepecki deems 'new dance' tendencies a direct legacy of the American minimalist movement in question.

than drama of psychological anguish, was intellectual complexity, something that had hitherto not been considered modern dance's — or women artists' — domain. (Banes, 1998:223)

Since Rainer's work, there has been a persistent line of dance that offers a predominantly intellectual contemplation on dance, rather than a spectacle of virtuosity and technique. This does not mean that all these practitioners necessarily chose 'not-dance'; rather, we could conclude that what has been unfolding since the 1960s in Western dance was a persistent, gradual, and mutual contamination of dance theory and practice. Importantly, ballet companies and dance work relying on technique and virtuosity did not cease to exist. In any case, ballet has its own history of changes and development (see Au, 2002; Morris, 2006) although it is usually considered to be a 'dead technique' stuck in nineteenth-century conventions of representation and beauty ideals. What happened instead is that there are almost parallel histories of Western theatrical dance that created difficulties in defining dance as well as in identifying a common field and methodology of research for dance scholarship. Furthermore, the history of dance usually places ballet at the historical beginning of Western theatrical dance forms, followed by modern dance, postmodern dance, and contemporary dance forms. In that sense contemporary dance is a historical successor of ballet If that is the case, however, how can we fully explain the existence of ballet today? To rephrase: if ballet was fully developed in the nineteenth century in the specific context of developing bourgeois society negotiating gender and class relations specific to that society, what is the source of enjoyment of ballet's 'dead technique' to the contemporary spectator when its original context has changed?

It is apparent that we should approach the question of dance technique here from a different angle: the question of dance technique cannot be resolved by claiming that dance technique simply reflects dominant gender and class relations of the original society. But what else is there? Judith Hamera partly answers this question and certainly puts the discussion in the right direction when she addresses the 'neglected aspect of virtuosity in dance':

> [There is a] highly allegorical, nostalgic activation of imagined, idealized relationships between the body and work abandoned by the relentless motility of capital, allowing audiences to view those vanishing modes with a romantic, backward glance. Some dance techniques generate this nostalgia by mystifying these relationships. Ballet soloists, for example, beckon spectators with the phantasmic possibility of artisanal ownership of one's labor through efforts so exceptional and so sublime they transcend even gravity. (Hamera, 2012: 752)

In this article Hamera was questioning the relationship between the virtuosity of Michael Jackson and the changing political economy of American work (2012:751–2). In the quotation above she points out, rightly to my mind, that the fantasy performed through ballet is less or not exclusively a gender fantasy but also the fantasy of labour. To further and expand on this debate I will address the accounts of my dancers on ballet and dance technique in general. Here again we should bear in mind the distinction between 'creative' and 'non-creative' work, maintained by them when speaking of ballet technique.

5. Dancers Speak of Ballet, Contemporary Dance, and Work

To Ziya ballet and dance technique in a more general sense[23] is completely irrelevant to capture the nature of the dance phenomenon. To him, dance technique is 'just technique' and anybody can master it (a 'trained monkey' can be a good technical dancer). Dance, to him, is about something 'more', about sending and receiving energy in communication with the audience. He is not predominantly interested in technique and when he 'discovered' Sufism he was not interested in creating a 'shocking', 'expressive', and 'impressive' dance vocabulary (Azazi, 2008a). In that sense, his turn to Sufism also marks a rejection of certain aspects of dance technique: Ziya believes in the 'healing' energy and power of dance and he does think that the fact that 'so many dancers refuse to dance today is kind of sad' (ibid., 2008a). In a sense, Ziya harbours the modern dance idea of the free body as opposed to 'technique' (the body oppressed by technique).

'Alexander's' views on the relation between contemporary dance and ballet are even more 'modernist' in appearance. He claims that for the mastery of contemporary dance it is much better if a dancer is not educated in any dance technique:

> Well, this style [meaning contemporary dance] of expression and functioning of the body in space relies more on setting it free from the burden that exists in ballet

---

[23] Ziya was the only one of my dancers that did not talk exclusively about ballet, but about dance technique in general. All other dancers somehow assumed the general discussion about dance technique to be about ballet.

and other dance forms and therefore it works better for uneducated dancers. I experienced that on my own skin when I attended some workshops in ballet school in Skopje. We had a multiple training programme there. First we had warming-up exercises which were not barre exercises like in ballet but derived from some technique of contemporary dance. I was much more successful in these exercises than those female pupils who had trained ballet for four years. ('Alexander', 2008)

This difference between 'creative' work of contemporary dancers and 'non-creative' work of ballet dancers is emphasized by a former Boston ballet dancer who claims that 'in ballet the dancer isn't really a creator ... You're there to dance. Not to think or suggest but just to focus ... you can get by being a superb technician and being entirely unthoughtful' (cited in Sussmann, 1990:24). A New York City ballet dancer adds: 'I don't know about ballet history and I don't care ... Ballet history is only words ... My style of dancing is what Balanchine wants me to do' (cited in ibid.:24).

Similarly, 'Peter' (who received formal ballet training) claims that ballet is competitive like sport, that it develops a non-reflexive, technically oppressed body. He dismissed ballet as 'just a job', boring and monotone, especially for ballet dancers who learn and execute the same steps for years. In his opinion, ballet dancers learn a repertoire once in their lives and then just endlessly execute the same steps. Note here how 'Peter's' view of a ballet dancer's work equates with factory work and alienated labour in a Marxist sense. Ballet dancers resemble factory workers, engaged in 'manual' and unreflective work that seems redundant under the new 'creative industries'. Ballet dancers, thus, do hard and alienating work, they are anonymous and oppressed by choreographers, theatre directors, and disembodied by the audience's gaze. Consequently, they do not do 'creative' work: there is no research in ballet — dancers just execute a timeless fixed score. This is not the place to assess the validity of these assumptions; rather, I propose to trace their origin. Ballet dancers appear as the opposite of the creative workers in creative industries. Ballet rehearsals rely on discipline, precision, and hard work (Wulff, 1998) and the mastering of technique takes years. Furthermore, 'Alexander's' account, when reflecting on the conditions of a ballet dancer's life and on ballet dance routine, clearly resembles Marx's theory of exploitation. When asked whether a contemporary dancer has more freedom (both in the sense of artistic self-development and in managing free time) than a ballet dancer, 'Alexander' responds:

> Yes I think so, because in contemporary dance, the dancer is not under pressure to have a particular diet or to maintain his weight. On the contrary, that is one of the contrasts between ballet and contemporary dance, because in ballet partnering includes lifting and then the female dancer has to watch her weight because her partner got used to it and every change in weight is putting them both in danger.
>
> Dunja: What about freedom in the performing sense?
>
> A: There is much more freedom in contemporary dance.
>
> D: And where do you think freedom lies in ballet?
>
> A: There is no freedom at all. Because even when you (the ballet dancer) finish rehearsing in a theatre it continues in your private life, which means that when you walk home you think about what are you putting in your mouth, how much should you sleep, that you have to wake up for warm-up, and then rehearse again. ('Alexander', 2008)

This account resembles Marx's ideas of exploitation in which labour takes the form of bodily expenditure (taking care how much you eat and sleep in order to work the next day) which must be replaced:

> The production of labour-power consists in [the worker's] reproduction of himself or his maintenance. For this maintenance he requires a certain quantity of the means of subsistence ... In the course of this activity i.e. labour, a definitive quantity of human muscle, nerve, brain, etc. is expended, and these things have to be replaced. Since more is expended, more must be replaced. (Marx, [1867] 1990:1275)

Marx's theory of exploitation heavily relies on the issue of body expenditure and embodiment. To Marx, both the humanity of man and life of his body are each, in turn, a function of work (see Bajorek, 2003). In *The Body in Pain: The Making and Unmaking of the World* (1985) Elaine Scarry argues, among other things, that the body is a physical basis of reality and, as such, it is something that can be made. For Scarry the making of the human body is the ultimate aim of artifice (Scarry, 1985:253). In this sense, Scarry offers a careful and in-depth reading of Marx's writing of embodiment and class relations, recognizing that his work relies on two interrelated assumptions. The first one is the presence of the body in the artefacts through the activity of 'making' and the second one is the making of the human body into an artefact (the presence of the artifice in the human body). These two interrelated assumptions make up the recognition that 'in making the world, man remakes himself' (ibid.:251).

However, what distinguishes the labouring class from the capitalist one is that the former cannot project itself in the realm of the artifice, i.e. while through the activity of making the labourer is exhaustingly 'engaged in the act of artifice, [he] is exiled from the realm of self-artifice' (ibid.:268). In short, while his/her body is making, he/she cannot *make* his/her own body since to Marx the sense organs such as skin and body tissue are themselves experienced through their own objectification. And since the worker lacks this objectification, he/she lacks his/her own body. Thus, Scarry summarizes this standpoint claiming that 'the problem of "the haves and have-nots" is inadequate to express its concussiveness, unless it is understood that what is had and had not is the human body' (ibid.:263).

If we follow this logic we may conclude that, shockingly, what a ballet dancer does not have is his/her body because while his/her body is making/producing all the time it cannot be objectified as a human body, since dancers are alienated from the system of production and reception of their work. Of course, the analysis so far is quite inadequate to describe the working conditions of contemporary ballet dancers, which have improved significantly, but it does serve to describe the horrific working conditions of late eighteenth- and nineteenth-century ballet dancers (see Robin-Challan, 1992). What we can infer for contemporary ballet dancers is that ballet is still a result of hard physical work, rather than that of artistic inspiration and talent, as shown in Wulff's ethnography of three ballet companies (1998).[24] Wulff terms ballet culture as that of 'injury and

---

[24] Helena Wulff in *Ballet Across Borders. Career and Culture in the World of Dancers* explores, cross-culturally, the occupational culture of ballet dancers from the anthropological and sociological perspective. Wulff conducted extensive fieldwork with the Royal Ballet in London, New York's American Ballet and the Royal Swedish Ballet.

pain', in which dancers communicate predominantly through their bodies.

There is, however, one more realm of tension between ballet and 'conceptual' work, or between 'creative' and 'manual' work in dance. As Laikwan Pang (2009) observed, the creative industry's mantra of workers' creativity and flexibility often disguises insecure job positions, lack of benefits, and so on (see also Murdock, 2002). This was powerfully conveyed by Igor from the opening remarks at the beginning of this chapter when he tries to communicate a lingering sense of insecurity inherent in the work of freelance dancers, where the power 'to conceptualize the reality' is coupled with exhaustion, insecurity, and fatigue.

The tension between the 'creative' work of the contemporary dancer and the 'body' work of the ballet dancer is no less maintained in the 'ballet world' as well. Wulff reports how less talented and technically less able ballet dancers usually become good contemporary dancers. Along the same lines, Foster claims that the 'inability to succeed at ballet implies failure at all dance' (Foster, 1997:243; also in an interview with 'Samir', 2009). In fact, there is a belief that contemporary dancers are just failed ballet dancers and ballet dancers label less talented colleagues 'thinking dancers' (Wulff, 1998:104), since they additionally learn steps from books and tapes (i.e. intellectually) and usually have to work more than their colleagues. Significantly, Wulff concludes:

> Connected to the contrast between 'thinking dancers' and those with 'natural talents' or 'good bodies' is the internal distinction between 'workhorses', who work very hard and can make surprising progress, and 'racehorses', who

do not have to work so hard, and yet find themselves on top, above the 'workhorses'. (Wulff, 1998:104)

The language that is used here through the distinction between 'workhorses' and 'racehorses' is important in questioning the (self) image that ballet dancers cultivate. Wulff's example portrays the ballet dancer as an animal, a noble animal (especially if you are a 'racehorse') but still, an animal. Felicia McCarren also draws attention to the nineteenth-century image of a ballerina as a racehorse but she also notes a change in this image:

> In the literature, paintings, and press of nineteenth-century Paris, the creature most often compared with the ballerina was the racehorse; like racehorses, ballerinas, were animal machines — fleet, swift, smooth. In the twentieth century, dancers became auto-mobiles: driven, motorized, mechanized. In a transition to a highly technologized world, dancers continued to be compared with finely tuned machines. (McCarren, 2003:2)

It is certainly in 'Peter's' narrative, especially in his recollections on his ballet education, that the image of a dancer as a machine prevails. His first memory of dance and movement was connected to the 'image of the gymnast' ('Peter', 2008) that he saw on television as a boy. He remembers being seduced by her 'mechanized and precise' but also 'beautifully synchronized and smooth' movements. Later, when he enrolled in ballet school to train as a dancer professionally, he developed highly negative attitudes towards ballet's rigorousness and 'machine-like aesthetic'. Another instance where dancers tended to connect their bodies (and) work with the machine is when speaking about ageing and a general feeling of fatigue. Ziya (born 1969) is the oldest of my dancers and was quite open about the impact of his 'ageing' body on his professional life. We discussed these issues at length when Ziya described how he cares for his body. This can literally be seen as careful body maintenance: on the one hand this included seeing his body as a temple in a spiritual sense, whilst on the other hand he was treating his body as a machine in the most utilitarian, dispirited way (Azazi, 2008b). 'Peter', similarly, revealed the major impact that a serious back injury had on his professional life, resulting in a change in career orientation. He stopped dancing and started working on cultural and dance management in his native Romania. He describes the reasons for his career change as follows:

> Last year, I was still dancing in one of my first productions 'Serial Paradise' which I created in 2003 and last year we had five or six performances in different cities: Amsterdam, Berlin, Rotterdam ... And I was really feeling like ... There is a moment when you do the lighting for the performance, when you do management, when you do performance; it is not possible anymore. So, I made the decision to stop dancing at least for a while ... Also my body is getting old and without the possibility of doing training every day it is impossible to continue working on so many projects. One has to travel, to always be getting on the plane, to adapt to different situations. ('Peter', 2008)

What is interesting in this quotation and what generally comes across in all the narratives of my dancers is the interconnection between issues of ageing, exhaustion, and a general feeling of fatigue. As seen from this quotation dancers are now multi-skilled 'total' workers. Their job descriptions include technical developments and regular rehearsals (technical demands for dancers have increased over the years); management and PR for their projects; and the constant mobility that requires immediate adaptation to new circumstances. Igor further elaborates these points:

> One is absolutely self-absorbed in his own work and there is no chance that you can genuinely work with other people through this kind of work. Of course, you can collaborate with someone, or have residencies but straight after one you have another project and there you go again ... I am a sort of person who likes to reflect and have enough time to process certain new experiences. Now, I am under the impression that I have less and less time and opportunities to sort out my own impressions. Now, I just go on with it with detached professionalism. I remember when I began this career how genuinely happy and excited I was when completing a good project. But now, I lost that excitement and it's nothing to do with age or maturity. Its literally ... you don't have time to ... it's just like working in the factory line where you take the bottle, pour the juice, put the cap on, and carry on with another bottle. It's very cruel somehow. (Koruga, 2013)

Igor's remarks conclude the discussion of this chapter in a significant way. They point to the fact, already indicated (Chapter Two), that there is a significant change in the modes of labour and production in contemporary dance — with the dissolution of stable fixed-salaried companies, dancers' labour became project-oriented, part-time with flexibility, which according to David Harvey (1989), became the modus operandi of late capitalism. There is also a significant caveat to be addressed here. 'Alexander's' remarks on the type of ballet work that resembles Marxist alienated factory labour, draws a distinction between ballet and contemporary dance across these lines (creative versus repetitive work). Igor, however, does not recognize this distinction. To him, all dancers are 'factory workers' ('just like working in the factory line') in the sense that all dance work is just that—work, and as such, does not escape management of labour in late capitalism.

6. Conclusion

In his *Empire and Beyond*, Toni Negri succinctly concludes that the main characteristic of the Empire (contemporary, late modernity) is the joining together of reason and affect in the very heart of production (Negri, 2008:67). Because of these changes in the modes of work and production, Negri concludes that compared with other immaterial labour, which is today hegemonic in producing goods and delivering services, the performing artist (theatre worker) 'has a primary dignity' (ibid.:218). I hope that, in this chapter, I have demonstrated why dance studies focusing on dancers' life patterns might provide an important contribution to the study of globalization. With regard to contemporary labour and society in general, the question is, of course, whether a Marxist (materialistic) analysis is appropriate. I will here draw on Jennifer Bajorek's conclusions in this regard. Bajorek (2003) addressed criticism which claims that Marx's theory is inadequate to theorize postindustrial society since the conditions of labour and capital have changed dramatically (see above). Bajorek underlines a particular aspect of this criticism connected to the machine. As her argument goes, the machine of Marx's times were doing what man could do himself (albeit faster, more efficiently, etc.), whereas the 'new generation of machines', which alters humanity, presupposes the machines that do what man cannot (computers, mobile phones, etc.). However Bajorek argues that dismissing Marx's theory as unable to encompass contemporary conditions of production dominated by this new kind of machine is a mistake: namely, this is 'already the world [Marx] describes in *Capital*. What is Capital but the supreme example of machine that does what man cannot?' (Bajorek, 2003:58). A second aspect of this critique is that Marx's theory of class relations is not adequate to address the complexity of contemporary social formations. Poststructuralism proved to be able to address this complexity but, in turn, it failed to account for production as a generator of signification (see Joseph, 2003). As Joseph remarked: 'Anybody can make a meaning, but not anybody can give that meaning efficacy in the world' (ibid.:26).

Returning to the question of labour we can understand why the question of production in dance is important and why the tensions between ballet and contemporary dancers and scholars are so heated. For if today, in the 'age of information', old factory machines collect dust in abandoned factories, why does dance technique still hold significance and fascination (and I refuse to conclude that these practices are regressive remnants of old times cherished by some sort of nostalgia)? How can we discuss dance technique and dancing bodies in relation to development of technology in the information society? I will provide tentative answers, approaching the question from different angles.

Firstly, Hardt and Negri's notion of the primacy of immaterial labour or 'thinking machines' over the 'body, manual, sweaty machines' is perhaps still too futuristic. We did not step out from the age of physical sweaty labour even if we acknowledge the ideological primacy of immaterial labour, as much as we believe we did. MacKenzie and Wajcman (1999) argue for the importance of the production in contemporary redefinition of labour much against Hardt and Negri's notion, asserting that:

> Production has not disappeared, but is being carried out in strikingly novel forms on an increasingly global basis. ... The quintessential product and symbol of the new age, the computer, is often manufactured in precisely this fashion. In the West there has indeed been a major shift of employment from factory work to service industries and office work, but much of this white collar work is an integral part of the production process and one in which technology plays a crucial role. (MacKenzie and Wajcman, 1999:141)

According to MacKenzie and Wajcman, not only do discourses of the social shaping of technology deserve our continuous attention, but also it is significantly important to pay attention to an entanglement of an increasing sophistication of technology and manual, physical work of Third World workers that produce its vital parts. Secondly, this entanglement between sophisticated technology and the manual 'sweaty' labour raised significant questions regarding (bio)technologies, dancing bodies, and dance labour. Considering these interrelations between dance and technology, dance scholar Kent De Spain marks growing anxieties within the dance community by asking:

> If 'humanity' is important, how will we define what is human and what is not in an era of increasingly extensive and invasive biotechnology? Will what is imaginable on the computer become what is demanded on a stage, and will the dancers who try to fulfil that vision be forced to resort to more and more radical assistance to improve or repair their overtaxed bodies? (De Spain, 2000:6)

Dance Performance as Production

What I am trying to say here is that there is a definitive paradox regarding the labouring body in contemporary 'cognitive' capitalism. On the one hand, there is an increased insistence on 'creativity' which is set against and set to conceal physical, body labour of dance. Even my dancers, despite the fact that their work is largely body-work, talk about the restrictive nature of dance technique (exemplified by ballet) and about the creative 'cognitive' research-based nature of their work. On the other hand, I showed how technical demands on dancers' bodies increased—dancers' bodies are now set to push boundaries of established dance technique by becoming even more daring, more virtuosic in what one English Royal Ballet dancer (Chapter One) calls 'almost like an evolution of mankind' (cited in Wainwright and Turner, 2004:325). This 'evolution' is closely connected to the developing biotechnologies and their impact on the very definition of sociality and humanity. Gilles Deleuze traces this notion albeit from a different angle. In writing on Foucault's idea of technology, Deleuze emphasizes that:

> The machines are social before being technical. Or, rather, there is a human technology which exists before a material technology. No doubt the latter develops its effects within a whole social field; but in order for it to be even possible, the tools or material machines have to be chosen by a diagram and taken up by the assemblages. (Deleuze, 1988:39)

Technologies are, thus, social, and social is essentially technological. Further, Donna Haraway in *Simians, Cyborgs, and Women* concludes that: 'Late twentieth-century machines have made thoroughly ambiguous the difference between natural and artificial, mind and body, self-developing and externally designed, and many other distinctions that used to apply to organism and machines. Our machines are disturbingly lively, and we ourselves frighteningly inert' (Haraway, 1991:152).

How are we to fight this inertia in our political and social lives? This question gets us back to the beginning of this chapter. Hardt and Negri's concept of the multitude, a new social class, that: 'In its will to be-against and its desire for liberation ... must push through Empire to come out the other side' (Hardt and Negri, 2000:218) as we have seen, received multiple criticism (Lotringer, 2003; Mertes, 2003; Wood, 2003). Furthermore, Catherine Lutz claims that many writings on Empire and the USA, including those of Hardt and Negri, neglect the ethnographic detail that would 'make the human face and frailties of imperialism more visible' (Lutz, 2006). We should examine the projects of the Empire in more detail—their vicissitudes on the ground, where people live—and die—for empire's sake' (ibid.:594). Ethnographies of contemporary imperial practices might draw attention to gender, racial, and ethnic qualities and differentiations of those practices and my work with dancers is oriented to those details.

Social lives of my dancers, as immaterial workers par excellence certainly display ambiguities inherent in concepts such as immaterial worker and the multitude when seen through the ethnographic looking-glass. The ambivalent but still strong relation of my dancers to a nation-state; their certain fragmented, non-coherent striving towards democracy, either through open criticism of global capitalism or more generally through dance as powerful mobilization and affective exchanges among bodies, show how fragile this new social class is in terms of defining a common ground of political action. Even the economic crisis of 2007 seemingly did not foster stories about resistance and anger but

Dance Performance as Production

emphasized that of survival within artistic and cultural sectors in respective nation-states. For instance, South East European dancers fight for funds and the survival of arts while Ziya Azazi contemplates a change of profession. These stories of survival mark what Tsianos and Papadopoulos see as 'a vacuum of protection' that characterizes contemporary immaterial work which is 'the almost existential condition of vulnerability felt as constant state of being in every moment of everyday life' (Tsianos and Papadopoulos, 2006:12).

Still, the investigation of dancers' lives has a great importance for understanding our contemporary political present not because they are paradigmatic examples of immaterial labourers but because they are living labour in general. Contrary to Hardt and Negri who emphasize the importance of immaterial workers in understanding contemporary labour and conceptualizing resistance, Tsianos and Papadopoulos assert that 'Deterritorialisation in post-Fordism cannot be conceived in relation to immaterial labour itself but in relation to the imperceptible experiences of the possibilities and oppressions pertinent to living labour' (ibid.:18). Tsianos and Papadopoulos contrast living labour to immaterial labour to chart what they term the condition of contemporary 'cognitive capitalism'. They claim, thus, that:

> The constitutive moment of contemporary system of production is not primarily its cognitive quality but its embodied realisation. In an attempt to overcome the somatophobia of the cognitive capitalist approaches we want to discuss the composition of living labour as an excess of sociability of human bodies. (Ibid.:19)

And this is where dance comes in as a paradigmatic example of living labour since dance's work is to create affective sociability and to transform the space in which it dwells.

This is not, again, to allocate to dance (performance) a certain by-default position of resistance, but to pave the way in which we can understand dance as living labour and living labour (its possibilities and oppressions) as the driving force of the contemporary form of capitalism. Thus conceived focus in dance studies will get us back to the question of the local in globalization, where the local does not disappear, but is in the process of constant transformation—the process of 'the packing in of global events, products, and frameworks into the local' (Friedman, 2001:57). Finally, the focus on the 'local' in the world of professional dance may illuminate the shaping cultural practices and formation of emerging identities as well as outline alternative political strategies of the future.

CHAPTER 5
CONCLUSION

1. A Few More Words On: Contemporary Dance and Global Mobility — Routes Versus Roots

The late twentieth century will be remembered as an age that put a definitive emphasis on mobility over stasis. As a consequence, Aihwa Ong noted that: 'Transnational mobility and manoeuvres mean that there is a new mode of constructing identity, as well as new modes of subjectification that cut across political borders' (Ong, 1999:18). The increased mobility has been theoretically connected with changes in the meaning of home and community (Di Stefano, 2002; Kennedy and Roudometof, 2003), new forms of labour (Salazar Parreñas, 2001; Smith and Favell, 2006), and new forms of identity (D'Andrea, 2007; Featherstone, 1995; Christiansen and Hedetoft, 2004). Discussing the changes in the modes of artistic labour, the theorist Bojana Kunst notes how contemporary artists are in the process of constant mobility that requires flexibility and generates a sense of uncertainty. Nothing seems to be stable and certain except project deadlines, and the sense of space is generated and experienced as a consequence of mobility (Kunst, 2010b:29). Dance studies developed a specific, if somewhat limited, take on the issue of dancers' mobility. For instance, a whole issue of the *Dance Research Journal* (2008) was dedicated to an investigation into the impact of immigration and mobility on dance under globalization. The issue in question contained several articles about dance revivals in immigrant communities and refugee camps across the world. These articles followed the globalization of dance forms and their impact 'back home' (Bosse, 2008;

Chatterjea, 2009; Hamera, 2002) as well as the historical impact of early twentieth-century immigration to the USA on modern American dance (Foulkes, 2000; Graff, 1997). These studies typically presupposed a clear separation between a ('back') home culture and a ('new') adopted culture which challenged dancers and dance forms in numerous ways. Sometimes this separation was seen as extremely dramatic such as in the case of the Cold War defection of Soviet ballet stars such as Rudolf Nureyev, Natalia Makarova, and Mikhail Baryshnikov. As David Caute noted: 'The ballet dancer's defection was the most spectacular of all: ovations, flowers, embraces—then, a flying "leap to freedom"'(Caute, 2003, cited in Scolieri, 2008:x). Although these studies are immensely important, there is an apparent lack of research concerning the mobility patterns of 'ordinary' professional dancers whose dance aesthetic cannot be seen as situated in the traumatic rupture between 'home' and 'adopted' cultures but rather perceived as a constant move across the globe. In short, the studies mentioned above treat dance as cultural currency, survival strategy, movement therapy, and social and political action. On the contrary, I wish to draw attention to the patterns of mobility in dance seen as a job and the dancer as a worker in the increasingly precarious creative industries.

Dancer Eleanor Bauer conducted her PhD research on a dance community in Brussels. In this research, she rightfully questioned and problematized the notion of 'community' not only as a result of globalization, a questioning which challenged the concept on numerous levels, but also, more significantly, due to the nature of dance work under globalization. Being a professional dancer herself, Bauer is in the privileged position to depict this new reality of dance work characterized by the constant move and complete lack

Conclusion

of separation between the private and professional lives of a dancer. Bauer writes:

> Now, when I look at my calendar and it appears more as a list of cities and countries than anything else, I am aware of that which I was not critical of before ... when 90 percent of my contact with friends and loved ones is online instead of in the flesh, I am aware of the chasm between social and professional needs that grows within such mobility. When 80 percent of my friends are in the performing arts field or are also professional relations, I am aware of conflation between the social and professional spheres that takes place in this field. When I pay rent and receive my mail in an apartment that I will only spend a total of two non-consecutive months in 2007, and when I only spend ten days a year in the city I call home; when the only place I have voting power (however fictional it may be) and pay taxes (however poorly they are spent) is a 24-hour commute away, and when I have people in three different cities asking me when I am coming home; when I have my own toothbrush in three other cities ... when my entire artistic career feels like it is on hold when my laptop is in the repair centre, making me realize that the new requirement for an artistic autonomy and productivity is no longer *A Room of One's Own* as Virginia Woolf would have it, but a Mac of one's own — a port for interconnection rather than a space for solitude ... I realize that I don't have to invent a performative answer to these issues — my life has become itself a performance of them. (Bauer, 2007:60)

Bauer's comments are very useful in understanding the mobility patterns of 'Peter', Igor, and especially Ziya who 'owns a toothbrush' in Vienna, Istanbul, and Grenoble. It is not only that there is no time and space left for private life outside the professional sphere, but there is less and less time left for rehearsals which not only results in a quicker creative process and a shorter lifespan for each project, but also in the massive strains and pressures put on dancers' bodies. This aspect of dancers' lives is not sufficiently discussed in the dance studies literature and certainly is not on the agenda of the creative industries (see MacNeill, 2009).

Moving away from the area of dance studies, dancers' lives and work patterns can significantly contribute to the globalization theories especially concerning the challenged notions of community and identity. Bauer herself is rightfully sceptical about the possibility of creating a 'dance community' as her research in Brussels reveals many reasons why the creation of the Brussels' dance community is under constant threat. She gives those reasons as follows:

> With less and less sustained structural support in general and more short term project support, the combination of an economy that wants star-figures and contains less long-term contracts is a double-blow to the collective. With no boss, no contract and an often unpredictable income, the maintenance of the collective requires the strong and persistent commitment of each participant who has to fight the currents of the freelance market pulling them into the undertow of the massive, individualistic, globe-trotting dance labor force. (Bauer, 2007:65)

A similar observation was made by Igor. When commenting on the similarities between dance scenes in Germany and Serbia, his account suggests that the world is 'truly globalized' because all dance scenes share a dose of precarity and threat:

> I realize that many predicaments that shake this dance scene [Belgrade], are also the problems in other scenes as well. Even in much bigger cities, the situation is similar; in

Conclusion

> New York it's similar; in Berlin it's similar. I've already mentioned how each year more and more students leave that school [University of Arts and HZT in Berlin—MA program Solo/Dance/Authorship, which Igor attended and completed]—where and how these artists are going to survive and work, no one asks. I mean there are always these stories circulating about how we should all connect and foster some initiatives, for instance, the independent scene in Berlin should gather and build up a strategy for collective action, but it cannot function. I mean ... Who are the actors on the independent scene in Berlin? It doesn't exist. I mean people are always in circulation and passing through, because everybody is always on the move in search for employment or because the lack of the appropriate visa, as in my case. (Koruga, 2013)

The idea of dancers as paradigmatic globe-trotters advanced by Bauer can be beneficial for the discussion of global hypermobility as an ascendant global condition that re-shapes existing forms of identity. With the call to study global hypermobility as an important predicament of globalization, I wish to emphasize that I regard this predicament as extremely paradoxical and contested. I believe that globalization is also a 'systemic process of closure and containment' (Shamir, 2005) that makes certain populations 'prisoners of geography' (Hausmann, 2001). This is also evident in Igor's account—there are predicaments shared by all scenes. But, at the end of the day, he is the one lacking an adequate visa. To develop this argument further, I will briefly return to the dance practices of two of my dancers, Ziya and Igor.

Igor struggles to develop his performance practice in both the local, Serbian context and 'international' German context. Currently, he is renting an apartment with a fellow dancer in Berlin and he struggles to sustain this lifestyle which is constantly 'in-between' these two cities. In discussing Belgrade-Berlin relations Igor remarked how Belgrade is a fixed spot in his life, whereas Berlin is flexible-moving. Everywhere else is just the places he visits through work. Within the 'fixed' context of Belgrade Igor connects with his family and long-term friendships that he tries to maintain in Belgrade. On the other hand, Ziya has a real 'life on the move', changing city and country approximately every fifth day. His practice is not grounded in a local context in which he tries to establish some sort of continuity. The communities he makes are the ones created in his workshops, and which he 'visits' approximately once a year. When asked what and/or where his 'home' is, he responded that there are certain emotions that he connects with home but that they are not bounded to a concrete geography.

To Ziya, due to his hectic, mobile life, home appears as an irretrievable loss and 'constant feel of homesickness':

> There is unfortunately no home for me. I say unfortunately because it would be much easier to have all the qualities of home in the same city, with the same people. ... But, this does not exist for me. I miss sometimes my childhood in Antakya for certain reasons, I miss Istanbul for certain reasons, I like Vienna for certain reasons, but I also miss cities that I visited in the past as all of them are part of the whole. But, in the meantime, I am not searching the solution for this homesickness. Because, this feeling is inside me and I will never find a solution. (Azazi, 2008b)

Ziya perceives his home as a landscape of emotions, connected with his regular activities (workshops, performances, rehearsals) and structures of time. With his feeling of loss connected with the notion of home, Ziya comes close

Conclusion

to what John Di Stefano calls 'the twentieth-century perpetual loss of home' (Di Stefano, 2002:39), a feeling that comes as a consequence of an increasingly transnational, mobile, and media-saturated world. To Igor, the question of home is deeply connected with some of the recent projects he is involved in. The topic of 'home', he admits, has been in his mind for a while. However, the situation is far from clear for him. When explaining about home he says:

> I like that question, because I am just about to go to Sweden to take part in the project that deals with the topic of 'home'. Even before, I found the topic interesting. I always like to joke about one great product of capitalism called Marina Abramović and her reference 'my home is where my body is', because I am always critical toward it as it implies some specific 'disembodied' form of cosmopolitanism. Personally, I find it hard to answer this question because I see my home as a 'base', a place I always return to. My current situation is that I live between Berlin and Belgrade and I cannot decide really where that is. Well, most of the time I'm in Berlin out of which I travel constantly. But I also return to Belgrade because of my health and therapy and I also have very close relationship with my family and with friends that I really treasure. I don't want to lose those because I changed my place of living. Those relationships are in a way 'home' for me and it's important for me to come to Belgrade as much as I can and keep in touch constantly. (Koruga, 2013)

In both cases there is a special way of negotiating local and global. In Igor's case his 'locality' is experienced mostly as marginality and gradual exclusion from the systems of funding and support he used to enjoy. His sense of mobility and connectedness with the outer, specifically the Western world is also negotiated with very concrete problems such as difficulties in obtaining a visa: so his 'local' is really experienced as 'other' than the 'global'.

Ziya's negotiating of the 'local' and the global is of a different nature to that of Igor's. He does not ground his practice in the small local performing scene nor has he material or legal problems with crossing borders. His 'locality' is thus negotiated through his inclusion of Sufism with which he managed to enter the 'local' of the 'global Sufism'. In this sense Ziya is revoking the local/global, East/West dichotomy only in the context of his performing practice. Igor is doing the same, although his experience of being grounded in the local and discriminately disconnected from the global makes his experience completely different. In Shamir's (2005) terms mentioned above, Igor experiences globalization as a 'systemic process of closure'.

In his *Global Nomads* Anthony D'Andrea (2007) traces new hypermobile identity forms by investigating a group of, as he names them, 'expressive expatriates' on the Spanish island of Ibiza and in Goa in India. D'Andrea suggests a 'dialogue between the anthropology of nomadism and philosophy of nomadology which would 'produce a theory of neo-nomadism as an ideal-type of postidentitarian mobility' (ibid.:24). In his study, D'Andrea tends to celebrate the sort of a-national character of these new identity formations. However, even when D'Andrea is at pains to connect 'nomad thought' with the practices of his 'expressive expatriates' as today's global nomads, his research shows that, unwittingly, any contemporary form of nomadism inevitably relates back to the state. Although neo-nomadic survival strategies include seasonal and part-time jobs more or less autonomous and expressive in nature they 'may also count on parental allowances, inheritance or state-based

Conclusion

unemployment support' (ibid.:222). Moreover, D'Andrea acknowledges that many expressive expatriates usually, as they get older, make efforts to legitimize their status in their adopted countries and generally display more anxieties connected to their precarious status.

Another important piece of research on global mobility and the dance profession is that of Janine Dahinden (2010) on cabaret dancers in Switzerland. Dahinden argues that cabaret dancers as genuine world travellers have to develop, to remain in circulation, a kind of mobility capital which involves, paradoxically, becoming 'sedentarized' to a certain degree in Switzerland. What Dahinden's study shows is that the gap between settled and circulatory migrants can be narrower than the studies of transnational migration usually suggest.

So far, I am inclined to concur with Dahinden and to suggest that the difference between 'settled' migrants and 'nomad' migrants is more a difference in degree than essential. From Eleanor Bauer's account discussed above it can be concluded that any form of nomadism (in this case the nomadism of professional dancers) depends not only on virtual networking with other nomads, but on concrete 'rootedness' in certain places ('having your own toothbrush' somewhere). In any case, the state is always already involved, especially with the case of the South East European dancers where their geopolitical location prevented them from developing professional dance careers with the mobility requirements of global contemporary dance markets.

2. 'Backstage Economies' and New Dance Methodologies

This book has told a story about the intersection between the practice of dance within the dance profession and the notion of cultural difference in the contemporary globalized world. It has also been a story about South East Europe after the fall of socialism, as these stories are intertwined. The story about globalization and/or South East Europe began with the war in the former Yugoslavia and other conflicts in Eastern Europe after the fall of socialism. Consequently 'an argument that evolved as an attempt to understand and respond to the conflict in South East Europe necessarily became an argument about global problems and possibilities' (Mostov, 2008:1–2). After the conflicts in the former Yugoslavia ended, the discussion on South East Europe ceased to exist outside the realms of economic and political policy making. South East Europe thus became neither a problem nor a possibility in the discussion and understanding of globalization.

The story about contemporary dance in South East Europe also started after the fall of socialism, and is strongly implicated in both the story about the unification of Europe and globalization as a wider process of creating a global culture and the dance market based on the recognition and respect for cultural/ethnic/gender differences (Savigliano, 2009). The main critical focus, which I explored from different angles in Chapters Two, Three, Four, and Five, is the notion of cultural difference that exists in contemporary multicultural politics and the ways in which this notion can be critically debated and challenged through a careful examination of its working in different socio-historical and geopolitical space(s). This critical examination was also intended to examine and broaden the field of dance studies. Firstly, the intention was to draw attention to the importance

Conclusion

of including dancers and their experiences in scholarly volumes. Secondly, the exploration of identity politics within the field of dance under globalization emphasized what Marta Savigliano (2009) calls 'World Dance' as a symptom of globalization:

> In World Dance the politics of identity and the ethic of difference translate as recognition and validation of aesthetics, pedagogies, and skills and even manners and motivations that are compatible (i.e. assimilable) to the established Dance field under the parameters established by Choreography. (Ibid.:185)

The question of 'World Dance' and a certain privileging of dance forms that document and celebrate cultural differences was the main focus of Chapter Two. It paid attention to the special role that cultural policies have in fostering these processes and the way local scenes struggle to negotiate these terms.

Chapter Four, on the other hand, pointed to the concern that the creative industries model failed to acknowledge the profound presence of the labouring bodies in the area of professional dance. This split understanding of dance as creative work and dance as body labour is also reflected in wider dance studies literature. Dance studies, as a part of the tradition of humanities and social sciences, is concerned with the aesthetical, cultural, and social aspects of dance, whereas dance as body labour is relegated to the realms of dance education and dance medicine (broadly understood as dance science). Therefore, there is a serious lack of understanding of the totality of dance labour, the everyday body-work of dance and interconnected issues such as body pain, injuries, and ageing. Yet, when speaking with my dancers these issues proved to be very significant.

Consequently, speaking and spending time with my dancers is not only what methodologically informed this book but it also enriched my own understanding of what the research is and should be about. In the introduction to this book (Chapter One), I have already outlined the call for dance scholars to embrace anthropology and its methodology which is strongest, for instance, in the writing of dance scholar Jane Desmond (see Desmond, 1993:2000). At the end of this book, however, I feel a need to launch this call myself. Anthropology has a special contribution to make to our understanding of transnationality by focusing on how an attention to everyday practices that constitute a dancer's life and the implicated relations of power can illuminate how the operations of globalization are translated into cultural and material logics that inform behaviour, identities, and relationships between people and things.

However, this is not a call to 'invade' one discipline with the methodological concerns and tools of another. What this book can conclude is that with the new modes of work and production in dance based on project-work and collaboration (Cvejić, 2005) and with the current line of questioning the ethic of (dance) writing, dance studies are themselves moving towards alternative research methodologies.

For instance, recently the political and ethical potential of dance practice and dance pedagogy became important considerations for both dance practitioners and dance scholars (Lewis, 2007; Mowitt, 2008; Peter, 2005). Valerie Briginshaw and Ramsay Burt edited the volume *Writing Dancing Together* (2009) in which they gave voice to topics related to the ethics of dance performance and dance creation, but they also raised a question of the ethic of writing (about) dance as a collaborative process. I have also argued already how the new generation of dancers

Conclusion

interested in Deleuzian philosophy and Spinoza's ideas of embodied ethics shape the new patterns of dance making and collaboration in European contemporary dance. Within the US field of dance studies, it was Randy Martin (1998) who forcefully connected dance with the political, developing the idea of dance as a reflective body practice that can serve as a model for the political mobilization of bodies. Along the same lines theorist Bojana Kunst claims that one of the main characteristics of contemporary cultural and economic relations is the so-called economy of proximity, which means: 'a shift from the autonomy and dynamism of movement to the broader social and cultural distribution of bodies' (Kunst, 2010a:85). Although Kunst was referring to changes in contemporary dance, this shift towards an ethics of performing and spectatorship is also characteristic of postdramatic theatre as discussed by Lehman (2002). Lehman argues that the specific quality of theatrical perception in postdramatic theatre is not only aesthetic but also entails an ethic of performing and spectatorship: 'In the reality of theatre itself the co-presence of actors and audience can make us aware that communication always means responsibility' (ibid.:76).

Finally, this 'economy of proximity' and the new modes of performance production mean that there is a demand that 'the dancer intervenes "apologetically" or "critically" in a given cultural or multicultural milieu, whereby dance is posited as a field of appropriation of culture' (Šuvaković, 2010:11). Seen like this, dance became an instrumental rather than an artistic practice — practice that 'critically reconstitutes social practices' (Lepecki, 2004a:1) and makes only 'limited references to history or cultures of dance' (Šuvaković, 2010:11). A dancer is now a researcher (Butterworth, 2009) — a philosopher, cognitive scientist, cultural critics and also artist, dramaturge, and PR manager. Given all these changes, it seems to me that some form of collaboration is appropriate, if not necessary, to inform theoretical writing. This might include interviews and workshop participation as well as spending time together sharing food, stories, and memories.

I spoke with my dancers in their kitchens, studios, offices, and then in the park, on the train, and in the coffee bars and restaurants. During my research dancers struggled with personal tragedies, insufficient funding, the rigours of touring, the general indifference of governmental institutions, and what they felt to be a constant feeling of threat. Dance scholar Joyce Morgenroth (2004) conducted research where she extensively interviewed twelve influential US choreographers letting them speak about their craft and private lives. My research differs from that of Morgenroth, beside other things, in my decision to focus on non-influential dancers and choreographers in my belief that 'small stories' may not have their proper place in the dance history, but are essential in understanding past and present dance industries. Lesley-Anne Sayers, when writing on ballet history from the perspective of the amateur ballet class exploring social history and cultural significance, summarizes my thought nicely: 'There are perhaps many histories of ballet that remain to be written, histories that have nothing to do with Sadler's Wells, the Ballet Rambert or the influence of Diaghilev. History that is of an industry, almost apart from the art form—but intimately related to its development' (Sayers, 1997:147).

Sayers thus shifted the focus from the ballet as high art and aesthetic tradition to the 'minor voices' of unknown amateur ballet dancers. This shift is a part of the larger re-orientation in dance studies that 'seeks authority not in

Conclusion

established figures and institutions but in voices of dancers, registering their themes and issues, discontents and contents, in what is ... an effort to create a balance between the researcher and "the researched"' (Meglin, 2000:139). Meglin underlines that this shift predominantly means that the object of analysis in dance studies shifted from elite and canonic dance forms, like ballet and modern dance, to the dance forms on the margins practised by subcultures and minorities in the society. As I underlined in Chapter Two, my research, although following this shift to listen to the 'minor voices' in dance industries, focused precisely on the canonical form of 'contemporary dance' in the societies that are 'not contemporary enough' (see Rowe, 2009), i.e. in the societies which are ideologically constructed as 'lagging behind' the West. This book argued that the production of 'contemporary dance' in the West and in not-quite Western societies is inevitably bound to geopolitical and social tensions and contradictions in the altered world of the twenty-first century transitional globalization (Šuvaković, 2010:11).

The close work with my dancers revealed how dance production in 'not-quite Western societies' (ibid.) is a potent laboratory for examining and revisioning the myriad complex interrelations between peoples, places, art markets, and competing aesthetics in globalization.

3. Postscript: Belgrade 2013

In September 2013 in Belgrade, I conducted what was to be my final interview for this book, which would appear in print in a matter of months. Igor, my interviewee dancer for the day, was explaining the profoundly exhaustive nature of his life as a freelance dancer. Humorously, he was describing his life as a constant rush for visibility and constant grant-application activities:

> Bojana Cvejić illustrated the situation correctly through the example of that cartoon character Wile E. Coyote chasing after the Road Runner ... and somehow that constantly rush for something ... Sometimes, it makes me wonder what exactly am I chasing after? What am I fighting for? I mean you are constantly in the mode of applying for something ... constantly writing applications. We were already talking about the kind of life this is ... Basically, you are getting off your parents' support to become dependent on some institutions which support you for the time being ... In fact, it's all very sad in a way. It's one profoundly lonely life, you are always on your own. (Koruga, 2013)

A thought struck me here suddenly. In 2007 when this research was at the beginning, the topic of artistic labour connected with 'new forms of capitalism' was almost non-existent, although there were some disparate voices that were beginning to tackle the topic tentatively (see Bauer, 2008; Kunst, 2010a). My own interest in artistic labour came from philosophers Hardt and Negri whose work, in a way, represents one the theoretical cornerstones of this book. A significant if discreet change that occurred in the last six years is that the question of artistic labour emerged with vigour. For instance, the latest issue of *Text and Performance Quarterly*, with a variety of responses from many performance studies scholars, saw a passionate discussion around issues of teaching, learning, and disseminating knowledge within performance studies and the conditions that makes these processes (im)possible. The issues in question framed the discussion at hand through 'solidarities

Conclusion

around day-to-day struggles of creating and maintaining performance studies praxis within often hostile institutions' (Terry, 2013:223). Although most of the articles referred to the censorship incident at the Villanova University, the underlying topic was certainly the issue of labour of performance either inside or outside the academy. In the same issue, for instance, Soyini Madison's essay most directly addresses these issues by, firstly, questioning the meaning of labour in performance and, secondly, by challenging 'performance people' (Madison, 2013:209) to re-think general conditions of labour that bring inexplicable suffering in the world. The Performance Studies international conference held in Leeds in 2012 also oriented its programme call around themes of economy, labour, and industry (Performance Studies international). Questions raised by the organizers were, for example: 'How much do we work per week?' and 'Where does the work end and life begin?' thus exploring shifts in performance industries and labour markets that influence the work and meaning of performance oriented work. In the 2012 special *PMLA* issue on work the editor, Vicky Unruh, directly relates its choice of topic with the 2008 financial crash that shook the international financial system (Unruh, 2012:733), while the 2010 issue of *Journal for Cultural Research* testifies to a remarkable rise in studies of creative and cultural labour in recent years (Hesmondhalgh, 2010:231). Finally, the 2012 special issue of *The Drama Review* raised the issue of labour in arts through the topic of 'precarity' and 'the political action regarding contemporary neoliberalism and the scene of performance-based art' (Ridout and Schneider, 2012:5). In the same year *Performance Research* issued a volume on labour and performance (Klein and Kunst, 2012), with the topics ranging from historical and discursive relations between labour and performance, to the impact of the austerity measures on the local dance scenes worldwide. It seems that the topic of artistic and academic labour is increasingly gaining in currency. Probably the most comprehensive book on labour in performance to date is Shannon Jackson's 2011 *Social Works: Performing Art, Supporting Publics*. Jackson questions the aesthetic autonomy of art in relation to intersecting social, political, and institutional economies. In line with Jackson, Judith Hamera's *Dancing Communities: Performance, Difference and Connection in the Global City* questions aesthetic and affective work of dance by looking at labour of dance technique in several dance communities in the Los Angeles area. In this study, as well as in her 2012 article, Hamera questions the relationships between technique, virtuosity, and the changing political economy of work in America. An interesting timeline is worth noting here. In the preface to the 2011 edition of *Dancing Communities*, four years after the first edition, Hamera gently re-frames the whole book through the recent threatening phenomena connected with commercialization of various world-making dance forms and practices (Hamera, 2011:xi). Her point is not to ponder on the difference between high art dance and its commercial, popular forms but to explore the points of their convergence: 'at the intimate coupling of dance and precarious' (ibid.:xii). There is a slight terminological convergence at play here as well: in four years, the term precarious and 'precariat' entered the general vocabulary of labour discourses especially in connection with artistic labour. Igor himself, when asked if dancers themselves and amongst themselves discuss the question of labour reiterated that dancers not only talk about it but they talk about it so much that it became almost like a 'fashion'. For instance, in the UK, it is the work of The Dangerologists, dance-theatre group

Conclusion

consisting of Broderick Chow and Tom Wells, who look at working life and labour through the prism of precarity. They explore these issues both through their performance work and through workshops and discussions. In Belgrade, Serbia, in November 2013, Slovenian dancer and performer Saša Rakef performed the piece called 'Saša Rakef's Debt' in which she tried to explore and probe into new dialogues about personal debt in order to understand global practical strategies in facing the debt crisis. Rakef's point of departure is her growing debt and blocked bank account as well as its influence on the dynamic of her everyday life. This move is significant—the problem of labour is suddenly very visible. However, it is worth noting that the way Igor talked about this 'trend' or visibility did not leave much room for optimism or change—this seems to be rather a bleak 'state of affairs'. This shift towards the visibility of the problem that nevertheless does not harbour its solution, is the shift, I believe, from crisis (in this instance global economic crisis) to normalization, a process that queer theorist Lauren Berlant calls 'slow death':

> The phrase slow death refers to the physical wearing out of a population and the deterioration of people in that population that is very nearly a defining condition of their experience and historical existence. The general emphasis of the phrase is on the phenomenon of mass physical attenuation under global/national regimes of capitalist structural subordination and governmentality. (Berlant, 2007:754)

The account of my dancers, especially in some more recent interviews (Azazi, 2012; Koruga, 2013), denotes exactly this 'wearing out': being constantly on the move but not getting anywhere; always working (if you are lucky, that is), but always earning 'just enough'; the feeling of exhaustion and health deterioration; and the feeling of helplessness. This statement was made towards the end of the interview with Igor:

> I don't want to appear to be constantly complaining. I like what I do. I like to do artistic work but the circumstances that allow me to do that are problematic. I understand the helplessness of an artist to change anything about it. He can swim through it and survive through sheer luck. (Koruga, 2013)

Perhaps adopting the notion of slow death at the end of this book is equally ample when writing about postsocialist/post-war societies and dance because the very term belongs not to traumatic events (performative rupture and crisis) but belongs to a space of ordinary life or environment to use Berlant's phrase:

> Slow death prospers not in traumatic events, as discrete time-framed phenomena like military encounters and genocides can appear to do, but in temporal environments whose qualities and whose contours in time and space are often identified with the presentness of ordinariness itself, that domain of living on, in which everyday activity; memory, needs, and desires; diverse temporalities and horizons of the taken-for-granted are brought into proximity. ... In an ordinary environment, most of what we call events are not of the scale of memorable impact but rather are episodes, that is, occasions that make experiences while not changing much of anything. (Berlant, 2007: 759–60).

This texture of ordinary life of 'ordinary' dancers was the topic of this book. In the introduction to this study, I have

Conclusion

briefly invoked Lyotard's observations on the event and everyday occurrences. In the same text Lyotard fleetingly compares events with nothingness and death, but he adds hastily to warn us that 'things are not so simple' (Lyotard, 1988:18). In this book I travelled the full circle to realize just that, and with Berlant's thesis on slow death, things indeed, are never simple. 'Backstage economies' of contemporary dance practices have illuminated, I hope, that all performance is social, to follow broadly Shannon Jackson (2011), as it depends on various social, political, and institutional economies. These economies often remain hidden in appreciation of artistic work and are also something that each artist unwittingly has to negotiate with. It is the dilemma that Igor has when placing his practice:

> I was always interested in collective, social situations to explore in my work and this is where my artistic allegiances lie ... The difficulties with this kind of work are: How to avoid community art? How to avoid communism that we have had in real socialism but not by becoming the opposite? These are the questions I will be grappling with all my life'. (Koruga, 2013)

BIBLIOGRAPHY

Adshead, J., ed., 1988. *Dance Analysis: Theory and Practice*. London: Dance Books.

Ahmed, S., 1999. Phantasies of Becoming (the Other). *European Journal of Cultural Studies*, 2(1), pp. 47–63.

Ahmad, A., 2008. *In Theory. Classes, Nations, Literatures*. London; New York, NY: Verso.

Ahmed, S., 2000. *Strange Encounters. Embodied Others in Post-Coloniality*. London; New York, NY: Routledge.

Albright, A., 1990. Mining the Dancefield: Spectacle, Moving Subjects and Feminist Theory. *Contact Quarterly*, 15(2), pp. 32–41.

Albright, A., 1997. *Choreographing Difference: The Body and Identity in Contemporary Dance*. Middletown, CT: Wesleyan University Press.

Albright, A., 1998. Techno Bodies or Muscling with Gender in Contemporary Dance. *Choreography and Dance*, 5(1), pp. 39–51.

'Alexander'. Personal interview. 5 Sep. 2008.

Amoore, L., 2002. *Globalization Contested: An International Political Economy of Work*. Manchester: Manchester University Press.

Appadurai, A., 1990. Disjuncture and Difference in the Global Cultural Economy. In: M. Featherstone, ed. *Global Culture: Nationalism, Globalization and Modernity*. London: Sage Publications, pp. 295–311.

Archetti, E., 1999. *Masculinities: Football, Polo and the Tango in Argentina*. Oxford; New York, NY: Berg.

Armstrong, T., 1998. *Modernism, Technology, and the Body: A Cultural Study*. Cambridge: Cambridge University Press.

Bibliography

Aronowitz, S., 1994. *Dead Artists, Live Theories, and Other Cultural Problems*. London; New York, NY: Routledge.

Asentić, S. and Vujanović, A., 2008. My Private Bio-Politics A Performance on a Paper Floor. *Performance Research*, 13(1), pp. 70–8.

Ashwin, S. and Lytkina, T., 2004. Men in Crisis in Russia: The Role of Domestic Marginalization. *Gender and Society*, 18(2), pp. 189–206.

Au, S., 1988 [2002]. *Ballet & Modern Dance*. London: Thames and Hudson.

Auslander, P., 1992. *Presence and Resistance: Postmodernism and Cultural Politics in Contemporary American Performance*. Ann Arbor, MI: University of Michigan Press.

Azazi, Ziya. Personal interview. 20 Feb. 2008a.

Azazi, Ziya. Personal interview. 13 Oct. 2008b.

Azazi, Ziya. Personal interview. 10 Apr. 2009.

Azazi, Ziya. Personal interview. 12 Nov. 2012.

BADco and De Campos 2012. Changes reprise. *Performance Research*, 17(6), pp. 112–15.

Badiou, A., 2005. *Handbook of Inaesthetics*. Translated by Alberto Toscano. Stanford, CA: Stanford University Press.

Bajorek, J., 2003. Animadversions—Tekhne After Capital/Life After Work. *Diacritics*, 33(1), pp. 42–59.

Balibar, E., 2003. Europe, an 'Unimagined' Frontier of Democracy. *Diacritic*, 33(3/4), pp. 36–44.

Banes, S., 1987. *Terpsichore in Sneakers*. Middletown, CT: Wesleyan University Press.

Banes, S., 1994. *Writing Dancing in the Age of Postmodernism*. Middletown, CT: Wesleyan University Press.

Banes, S., 1998. *Dancing Women: Female Bodies on Stage*. London: Routledge.

Baudrillard, J., 1981. *For a Critique of the Political Economy of the Sign*. Translated by Charles Levin. St. Louis, MO: Telos Press.

Bauer, B., 2008. The Makings of...Production and Practice of the Self in Choreography: The Case of Vera Mantero and Guests. *Performance Research*, 13(1), pp. 15-22.

Bauer, E., 2007. Becoming Room, Becoming Mac: New Artistic Identities in the Transnational Brussels Dance Community. *Maska*, 107-8, pp. 58-67.

Berlant, L., 2007. Slow Death (Sovereignty, Obesity, Lateral Agency). *Critical Inquiry*, 33(4), pp. 754-80.

Bhabha, H., 1994. *The Location of Culture*. London: Routledge.

Birringer, J., 2003. A New Europe. *PAJ: A Journal of Performance and Art 75*, 25(3), pp. 26-41.

Birringer, J., 2005. Dance and Not Dance. *PAJ: A Journal of Performance and Art, 80*, 27(2), pp. 10-27.

Bjelić, D., 2006. The Balkans: Europe's Cesspool. *Cultural Critique*, 62, pp. 33-66.

Bodman, H. and Tohidi, N. eds., 1998. *Women in Muslim Societies. Diversity within Unity*. Boulder, CO: Lynne Rienner Publishers.

Boltanski, L. and Chiapello, È., 2005. The New Spirit of Capitalism. *International Journal of Politics, Culture, and Society*, 18 (3/4), pp. 161-88.

Boon, V. and Delanty, G., 2007. Cosmopolitanism and Europe: Historical Considerations and Contemporary Applications. In: C. Rumford, ed. *Cosmopolitanism and Europe*. Liverpool: Liverpool University Press, pp. 19-39.

Böse, M., Busch, B., and Dragićević Šešić, M., 2006. Despite and Beyond Cultural Policy: Third and Fourth-Sector Practices and Strategies in Vienna and Belgrade. In: U. Meinhof and A. Triandafyllidou, eds. *Transcultural*

Bibliography

Europe: Cultural Policy in a Changing Europe. Basingstoke: Palgrave Macmillan, pp. 131-57.

Bosse, J., 2008. Salsa Dance and the Transformation of Style: An Ethnographic Study of Movement and Meaning in a Cross-Cultural Context. *Dance Research Journal*, 40(1), pp. 45-64.

Bourdieu, P., 1993. *The Field of Cultural Production: Essays on art and Literature*. R. Johnson, ed. Cambridge: Polity Press.

Bradbury, M., 1995. What was Post-Modernism? The Arts in and after the Cold War. *International Affairs*, 71(4), pp. 763-74.

Brennan, T., 2004. *The Transmission of Affect*. Ithaca, NY: Cornell University Press.

Briginshaw, V. and Burt, R. eds., 2009. *Writing, Dancing Together*. Basingstoke: Palgrave Macmillan.

Bryson, N., 1997. Cultural Studies and Dance History. In: J. Desmond, ed. *Meaning in Motion: New Cultural Studies of Dance*. Durham, NC, London: Duke University Press, pp. 55-77.

Burt, R., 1995. *The Male Dancer: Bodies, Spectacle, Sexualities*. New York, NY: Routledge.

Burt, R., 2000. Dance Theory, Sociology and Aesthetic. *Dance Research Journal*, 32(1), pp. 125-31.

Butterworth, J., 2009. Choreographer as Researcher: Issues and Concepts in Postgraduate Study. In: J. Butterworth, and L. Wildschut, eds. *Contemporary Choreography: A Critical Reader*. London; New York, NY: Routledge, pp. 152-71.

Carlson, M., 2004. *Performance: A Critical Introduction*. London; New York, NY: Routledge.

Carr, M., 2012. *Fortress Europe: Dispatches from a Gated Continent*. New York, NY: The New Press.

Carter, A., 2004a. Introduction. In: A. Carter, ed. *Rethinking Dance History: A Reader*. London: Routledge, pp. 1–10.

Carter, A., 2004b. Destabilizing the Discipline: Critical Debates about History and their Impact on the Study of Dance. In: A. Carter, ed. *Rethinking Dance History: A Reader*. London: Routledge, pp. 10–20.

Case, S., Brett, P., and Foster, S., eds., 1995. *Cruising the Performative: Interventions into the Representation of Ethnicity, Nationality and Sexuality*. Bloomington, IN: Indiana University Press.

Cash, J., 2007. The Social Role of Artists in Post-Soviet Moldova: Cultural Policy, Europeanisation, and the State. Europe-Asia Studies, 59(8), pp. 1405–27.

Castells, M., 1996. *The Rise of the Network Society*. Cambridge, MA; Oxford: Blackwell Publishers.

Cerwonka, A., 2008. Traveling Feminist Thought: Difference and Transculturation in Central and Eastern European Feminism. *Signs: Journal of Women in Culture and Society*, 33(4), pp. 809–32.

Chatterjea, A., 2009. Red-stained Feet: Probing the Ground on which Women Dance in Contemporary Bengal. In: S. Foster, ed. *Worlding Dance*. Basingstoke: Palgrave Macmillan, pp. 119–44.

Chioni Moore, D., 2001. Is the Post- in the Postcolonial the Post- in the Post-Soviet? Towards the Global Postcolonial Critique. *PMLA*, 116(1), pp. 111–28.

Chowdhury, K., 2006. Interrogating 'Newness': Globalization and Postcolonial Theory in the Age of Endless War. *Cultural Critique*, 62, pp. 126–61.

Christiansen, F. and Hedetoft, U. eds., 2004. *The Politics of Multiple Belonging: Ethnicity and Nationalism in Europe and East Asia*. Aldershot: Ashgate Publishing.

Bibliography

Clark, A., 2008. Pressing the Flesh: A Tension in the Study of the Embodied, Embedded Mind? *Philosophy and Phenomenological Research*, 76(1), pp. 37-59.

Cohen, R., 1987. *Theatre of Power: The Art of Diplomatic Signalling*. London: Longman Group United Kingdom.

Comacchio, C., 1998. Mechanomorphosis: Science, Management, and 'Human Machinery' in Industrial Canada, 1900-45. *Labour/Le Travail*, 41, pp. 35-67.

Cook, I. and Harrison, M., 2003. Cross Over Food: Re-materializing Postcolonial Geographies. *Transactions of the Institute of British Geographers*, 28(3), pp. 296-317.

Copeland, R., 1998. Between Description and Deconstruction. In: A. Carter, ed. *The Routledge Dance Studies Reader*. London; New York, NY: Routledge, pp. 98-108.

Copeland, R. and Cohen, M., eds., 1983. *What is Dance*. Oxford: Oxford University Press.

Cowan, J., 1990. *Dance and the Body Politic in Northern Greece*. Princeton, NJ: Princeton University Press.

Cvejić, B., 2002. I.N.T.R.A.D.A. *TKH – Journal for Performing Arts Theory*, 4, pp. 5-7.

Cvejić, B., 2005. Collectivity? You Mean Collaboration. Available at: www.republicart.net [Accessed 13 March 2013].

Cvejić, B., 2007. Learning by Making (Contemporary Choreography in Europe: When did Theory Give Way to Self-organization?). Available at:
http://www.lanimal.org/image/memoria/175/pdf/080401-175-2.pdf [Accessed 12 February 2013].

Dahinden, J., 2010. Cabaret Dancers: 'Settle Down in Order to Stay Mobile?' Bridging Theoretical Orientations within Transnational Migration Studies. *Social Politics:*

International Studies in Gender, State and Society, 17(3), pp. 323–48.

Daly, A., 1987. The Balanchine Woman: Of Hummingbirds and Channel Swimmers. *The Drama Review: TDR*, 31(1), pp. 8–21.

D'Amelio, T., 2008. On the Premises of French Contemporary Dance: Concepts, Collectivity and 'Trojan Horses' in the Work of Jérôme Bel and Loïc Touzé. In: J. Lansdale, ed. *Decentring Dancing Texts. The Challenge of Interpreting Dances*. Palgrave Macmillan, pp. 89–107.

D'Andrea, A., 2007. *Global Nomads: Techno and New Age as Transnational Countercultures in Ibiza and Goa*. London; New York, NY: Routledge.

Deleuze, G., 1988. *Foucault*. Translated by Sean Hand. Minneapolis, MN: Minnesota University Press.

Deleuze, G., 1994. *Difference and Repetition*. Translated by Paul Patton. New York: Columbia University Press.

Desmond, J., 1993. Embodying Difference: Issues in Dance and Cultural Studies. *Cultural Critique*, 26, pp. 33–63.

Desmond, J., 2000. Terra Incognita: Mapping New Territory in Dance and 'Cultural Studies'. *Dance Research Journal*, 32(1), pp. 43–53.

Desmond, J., ed., 2001. *Dancing Desires: Choreographing Sexualities On and Off the Stage*. Madison, WI: University of Wisconsin Press.

De Spain K., 2000. Dance and Technology: A Pas de Deux for Post-Humans. *Dance Research Journal*, 32(1), pp. 2–17.

Dirlik, A., 1998. *The Postcolonial Aura: Third World Criticism in the Age of Global Capitalism*. Boulder, CO; Oxford: Westview.

Di Stefano, J., 2002. Moving Images of Home. *Art Journal*, 61(4), pp. 38–51.

Bibliography

Dragićević-Šešić, M., and Dragojević, S., 2006. Imagined or Real Divides? In: U. Meinhof and A. Triandafyllidou, eds. *Transcultural Europe: Cultural Policy in a Changing Europe*. Basingstoke: Palgrave MacMillan, pp. 43–57.

Ducatel, K., Webster, J., and Hermann, W., eds., 2000. *The Information Society in Europe: Work and Life in an Age of Globalization*. Lanham, MD: Rowman & Littlefield Publishers.

Einhorn, B., 1993. *Cinderella Goes to Market: Citizenship, Gender and Women's Movements in East Central Europe*. London: New York, NY: Verso.

Eley, G., 2007. Historicizing the Global, Politicizing Capital: Giving the Present a Name. *History Workshop Journal*, 63, pp. 154–88.

Farnell, B., 1994. Ethno-Graphics and the Moving Body. *Man: Journal of the Royal Anthropological Institute*, 29(4), pp. 929–74.

Featherstone, M., 1995. *Undoing Culture: Globalization, Postmodernism, Identity*. Newbury Park, CA: Sage.

Forrester, S., Zaborovska, M., and Gapova, E., 2004. Introduction. In: S. Forrester, M. Zaborovska, and E. Gapova, eds. *Over the Wall/After the Fall: Post-Communist Cultures Through an East-West Gaze*. Bloomington, IN: Indiana University Press.

Foster, S., 1986. *Reading Dancing: Bodies and Subjects in Contemporary American Dance*. Berkeley, CA: University of California Press.

Foster, S., 1996a. *Corporealities: Dancing, Knowledge, Culture, and Power*. Abingdon: Psychology Press.

Foster, S., 1996b. *Choreography and Narrative. Ballet's Staging of Story and Desire*. Bloomington and Indianapolis, IN: Indiana University Press.

Foster, S., 1997. Dancing Bodies. In: J. Desmond, ed. *Meaning in Motion: New Cultural Studies of Dance*. Durham, NC; London: Duke University Press, pp. 235-57.

Foster, S., 1998. Choreographies of Gender. *Signs*, 24(1), pp. 1-33.

Foucault, M., 1991. *Discipline and Punish: The Birth of the Prison*. Translated by Alan Sheridan. Harmondsworth: Penguin.

Foulkes, J., 2000. Angels 'Revolt!': Jewish Women in Modern Dance in the 1930s. *American Jewish History*, 88(2), pp. 233-52.

Foulkes, J., 2001. Dance is for American Men: Ted Shawn and the Intersection of Gender, Sexuality, and Nationalism in the 1930s. In: J. Desmond, ed. *Dancing Desires: Choreographing Sexualities On and Off the Stage*. Madison, WI: University of Wisconsin Press, pp. 113-47.

Fox, C., 1994. The Portable Border: Site-Specificity, Art, and the U.S.—Mexico Frontier. *Social Text*, 41, pp. 41-62.

Franko, M., 1993. *Dance as Text: Ideologies of the Baroque Body*. Cambridge: Cambridge University Press.

Franko, M., 1995. *Dancing Modernism/Performing Politics*. Bloomington, IN: Indiana University Press.

Franko, M., 2002. *The Work of Dance: Labor, Movement, and Identity in the 1930s*. Middletown, CT: Wesleyan University Press.

Friedman, J., 2001. Indigenous Struggles and the Discreet Charm of the Bourgeoisie. In: R. Prazniak and A. Dirlik, eds. *Places and Politics in an Age of Globalization*. New York, NY; Oxford: Rowman & Littlefield Publishers, pp. 53-73.

Gal, S. and Kligman, G., 2000. *The Politics of Gender After Socialism: A Comparative-Historical Essay*. Princeton, NJ; Chichester: Princeton University Press.

Bibliography

Garafola, L., 1985. The Travesty Dancer in Nineteenth-Century Ballet. *Dance Research Journal*, 17(2), pp. 35–40.

Gard, M., 2006. *Men Who Dance: Aesthetic, Athletic & Art of Masculinity*. New York, NY: Peter Lang Publishing.

Gardner, S., 2007. Dancer, Choreographer and Modern Dance Scholarship. *Dance Research: The Journal of the Society for Dance Research*, 25(1), pp. 35–53.

Giersdorf, J., 2009. Dance Studies in the International Academy: Genealogy of a Disciplinary Formation. *Dance Research Journal*, 41(1), pp. 23–44.

Gikandi, S., 2000. Globalization and the Claims of Postcoloniality. *South Atlantic Quarterly*, special issue on Globalization and Anglophone Literature, 98(1), pp. 625–56.

Gille, Z. and Ó Riain, S., 2002. Global Ethnography. *Annual Review of Sociology*, 28, pp. 271–95.

Golubović, Z., 2006. Pouke i dileme minulog veka. [Lessons and dilemmas of the past century]. Beograd: Filip Višnjić.

Gómez-Peña, G., 1996. *The New World Border: Prophecies, Poems & Loqueras for the End of the Century*. San Francisco, CA: City Lights Books.

Gordon, S., 1984. *Off Balance: The Real World of Ballet*. New York, NY: McGraw-Hill.

Graff, E., 1997. *Stepping Left: Dance and Politics in New York City, 1928–1942*. Durham, NC: Duke University Press.

Grau, A., 1994. Feminist Ethnography and Performance. *Dance Research: The Journal of the Society for Dance Research*, 12(1), pp. 12–20.

Green, J., 1999. Somatic Authority and the Myth of the Ideal Body in Dance Education. *Dance Research Journal*, 31(2), pp. 80–100.

Gržinić, M., 2009. From Biopolitics to Necropolitics. Available at: http://www.old.tkh-generator.net/en/openedsource/from-biopolitics-to-necropolitics-0 [Accessed 10 December 2013].

Gupta, A. and Ferguson, J., 1992. Beyond "Culture": Space, Identity, and the Politics of Difference. *Cultural Anthropology*, 7(1), pp. 6–23.

Hamera, J., 2002. An Answerability of Memory: 'Saving' Khmer Classical Dance. *TDR: The Drama Review*, 46(4), pp. 65–85.

Hamera, J., 2007. *Dancing Communities: Performance, Difference, and Connection in the Global City*. Basingstoke: Palgrave Macmillan.

Hamera, J., 2011. *Dancing Communities: Performance, Difference, and Connection in the Global City*. 2nd edition. Basingstoke: Palgrave Macmillan.

Hamera, J., 2012. The Labors of Michael Jackson: Virtuosity, Deindustrialization, and Dancing Work. *PMLA*, 127(4), pp. 751–65.

Hammond, P. and Hammond, S., 1979. The Internal Logic of Dance: A Weberian Perspective on the History of Ballet. *Journal of Social History*, 12(4), pp. 591–609.

Hanna, J. L., 1987. Patterns of Dominance: Men, Women, and Homosexuality in Dance. *TDR: The Drama Review*, 31(1), pp. 22–47.

Hanna, J. L., 1988. *Dance, Sex and Gender*. Chicago, IL: University of Chicago Press.

Haraway, D., 1991. *Simians, Cyborgs, and Women: The Reinvention of Nature*. New York, NY: Routledge.

Hardt, M. and Negri, A., 2000. *Empire*. Cambridge, MA: Harvard University Press.

Hardt, M. and Negri, A., 2004. *Multitude: War and Democracy in the Age of Empire*. New York, NY: The Penguin Press.

Bibliography

Harvey, D., 1989. *The Condition of Postmodernity: An Enquiry into the Origins of Cultural Change.* Oxford; Cambridge, MA: Blackwell.

Hausmann, R., 2001. Prisoners of Geography. *Foreign Policy,* January, pp. 44–53.

Head, S., 2003. *The New Ruthless Economy: Work and Power in the Digital Age.* Oxford: Oxford University Press.

Herzfeld, M., 2005. *Cultural Intimacy: Social Poetics in the Nation-State.* New York, NY; London: Routledge.

Hesmondhalgh, D., 2010. Normativity and Social Justice in the Analysis of Creative Labour. *Journal for Cultural Research,* 14(3), pp. 231–49.

Hewitt, A., 2005. *Social Choreography. Ideology as Performance in Dance and Everyday Movement.* Durham, NC; London: Duke University Press.

Howe, D., 1996. *Individuality and Expression: The Aesthetic of the New German Dance, 1908–1936.* New York, NY: Peter Lang.

Howell, R., 1975. The USSR: Sport and Politics Intertwined. *Comparative Education,* 11(2), pp. 137–45.

Innes, S., 1988. The Teaching of Ballet. *Writings on Dance,* 3, pp. 37–47.

'Ivan'. Personal Interview. 15 Jan. 2009.

Jackson, N., 1994. Dance Analysis in Publications of Janet Adshead and Susan Foster. *Dance Research: The Journal of the Society for Dance Research,* 12(1), pp. 3–11.

Jackson, S., 2011. *Social Works: Performing Arts, Supporting Publics.* London; New York: Routledge.

Jaffe Robbins, S., 1994. Review: Postcommunist, Prefeminist? *The Women's Review of Books,* 11(12), pp. 26–7.

Jameson, F., 1979. Reification and Utopia in Mass Culture. *Social Text,* 1, pp. 130–48.

Jameson, F., 1991. *Postmodernism, or, the Cultural Logic of Late Capitalism*. London: Verso.
Jameson, F., 1994. *The Seeds of Time*. New York, NY: Columbia University Press.
Jameson, F., 1998. *The Cultural Turn: Selected Writings on Postmodern, 1983-1988*. London; New York, NY: Verso.
Jansen, S., 2009. After the Red Passport: Towards an Anthropology of the Everyday Geopolitics of Entrapment in the EU's Immediate Outside. *Journal of the Royal Anthropological Institute*, 15(4), pp. 815-32.
Joseph, M., 2003. The Performance of Production and Consumption. In: P. Auslander, ed. *Performance: Critical Concepts in Literary and Cultural Studies*. London; New York, NY: Routledge, Vol. 3, pp. 372-405.
Jovanović, M. and Naumović, S. eds., 2001. *Gender Relations in South Eastern Europe. Historical Perspectives on Womanhood and Manhood in 19th and 20th Century*. Belgrade, Graz: Zur Kunde Südosteuropas Band II/33 and Udruženje za Društvenu Istoriju, IDEJE 4.
Kagitcibasi, C., 1986. Status of Women in Turkey: Cross-Cultural Perspectives. *International Journal of Middle East Studies*, 18(4), pp. 485-99.
Kennedy, P. and Roudometof, V. eds., 2003. *Communities Across Borders: New Immigrants and Transnational Cultures*. London; New York, NY: Routledge.
Keough, L., 2006. Globalizing 'Postsocialism': Mobile Mothers and Neoliberalism on the Margins of Europe. *Anthropological Quarterly*, 79(3), pp. 431-61.
Kiwan, S. N. and Kosnick, K., 2006. Perspectives on Cultural Diversity: A Discourse Analytical Approach. In: U. Meinhof and A. Triandafyllidou, eds. *Transcultural Europe: Cultural Policy in a Changing Europe*. Basingstoke: Palgrave MacMillan, pp. 57-81.

Bibliography

Kiwan, S. N. and Meinhof, U., 2006. Perspectives on Cultural Diversity: A Discourse Analytical Approach. In: U. Meinhof and A. Triandafyllidou, eds. *Transcultural Europe: Cultural Policy in a Changing Europe*. Basingstoke: Palgrave MacMillan, pp. 105–30.

Klein, G. and Kunst, B., 2012. Introduction: Labour and Performance. *Performance Research*, 17(6), pp. 1–2.

Kompridis, N., 2005. Normativizing Hybridity/ Neutralizing Culture. *Political Theory*, 33(3), pp. 318–43.

Kondo, D., 1990. *Crafting Selves: Power, Gender, and Discourses of Identity in a Japanese Workplace*. Chicago, IL: University of Chicago Press.

Koritz, A., 1996. Re/Moving Boundaries. From Dance History to Cultural Studies. In: G. Morris, ed. *Moving Words: Re-writing Dance*. London: Routledge, pp. 88–107.

Koruga, Igor. Personal Interview. 27 Sep. 2013.

Kristeva, J., 2000. *Crisis of the European Subject*. New York, NY: Other Press, pp. 163–83.

Kunst, B., 2002. Performing the Other/Eastern Body. Available at www.kunstbody.org [Accessed 20 November 2010].

Kunst, B., 2010a. The Economy of Proximity. *Performance Research*, 14(3), pp. 81–8.

Kunst, B., 2010b. Prognosis on Collaboration. *Joint issue of Le Journal des Laboratoires and TKH – Journal for Performing Arts*, 17, pp. 23–9.

Kurt, B., 2008. Analysis of Prejudices against the Male Dancer in the Case of 'Sinop Köçeks'. *Dance Ethnography Forum*, De Montfort University, Leicester, United Kingdom, January 2008.

Lehman, H. T., 2002. The Political in the Post-Dramatic. *Maska*, 17(74–5), pp. 61–72.

Lepecki, A., 2004a. Inscribing Dance. In: A. Lepecki, ed. *Of the Presence of the Body: Essays on Dance and Performance Theory*. Hanover, NH: Wesleyan University Press, pp. 124–40.

Lepecki, A., 2004b. Concept and Presence: The New European Dance Scene. In: A. Carter, ed. *Rethinking Dance History: A Reader*. London: Routledge, pp. 170–82.

Lepecki, A., 2006a. Mutant Enunciations. *TDR: The Drama Review*, 50(4), pp. 17–20.

Lepecki, A., 2006b. *Exhausting Dance: Performance and Politics of Movement*. New York, NY: Routledge.

Le Roy, X., n.d. Self Interview. Available at www.insituproductions.net/_eng/frameset.html [Accessed 20 January 2009].

Lesage, D., 2012. Permanent Performance. *Performance Research*, 17(6), pp. 14–21.

Levy, D. and Sznaider, N., 2007. Memories of Europe: Cosmopolitanism and Its Others. In: C. Rumford, ed. *Cosmopolitanism and Europe*. Liverpool: Liverpool University Press, pp. 158–81.

Lewis, T., 2007. Philosophy — Aesthetics — Education: Reflections on Dance. *The Journal of Aesthetic Education*, 41(4), pp. 53–66.

Lock, M., 1993. Cultivating the Body: Anthropology and Epistemologies of Bodily Practice and Knowledge. *Annual Review of Anthropology*, 22, pp. 133–55.

Lotringer, S., 2003. Introduction. *A Grammar of the Multitude: For an Analysis of Contemporary Forms of Life*. Cambridge MA; London: Semiotext(e).

Lotringer, S., 2005. We, the Multitude. *Social Text*, 82, 23(1), pp. 1–14.

Lutz, C., 2006. Empire is in the Details. *American Ethnologists*, 33(4), pp. 593–611.

Bibliography

Lyotard, J., 1988. *Peregrinations: Law, Form, Event*. New York, NY: Columbia University Press.

McCarren, F., 2003. *Dancing Machines. Choreographies of the Age of Mechanical Reproduction*. Stanford, CA: Stanford University Press.

McDowell, L., 2009. *Working Bodies: Interactive Service Employment and Workplace Identities*. Chichester: Wiley-Blackwell.

MacKenzie, D. and Wajcman, J., 1999. *The Social Shaping of Technology*. Buckingham; Philadelphia, PA: Open University Press.

McKenzie, J., 2001. *Perform or Else: From Discipline to Performance*. London: Routledge.

McLellan, D., ed., 1971. *Marx's Grundrisse*. London; Basingstoke: Palgrave Macmillan.

McNally, D., 2001. *Bodies of Meaning: Studies in Language, Labor and Liberation*. Albany, NY: State University of New York Press.

MacNeill, K., 2009. Pina Bausch, Creative Industries and the Materiality of Artistic Labour. *International Journal of Cultural Policy*, 15(3), pp. 301–13.

Madison, S., 2013. That Was Then and This is Now. *Text and Performance Quarterly*, 33(3), pp. 207–11.

Malefyt, T., 1998. "Inside" and "Outside" Spanish Flamenco: Gender Constructions in Andalusian Concepts of Flamenco Tradition. *Anthropological Quarterly*, 71(2), pp. 63–73.

Manning, S., 1988. Review: Modernist Dogma and Post-Modern Rhetoric: A Response to Sally Banes's "Terpsichore in Sneakers". *TDR: The Drama Review*, 32(4), pp. 32–9.

Marciniak, K., 2009. Post-Socialist Hybrids. *European Journal of Cultural Studies*, 12(2), pp. 173–90.

Marcus, G., 1995. Ethnography in/of the World System: The Emergence of Multi-Sited Ethnography. *Annual Review of Anthropology*, 24, pp. 95–117.

Martin, J., 1980. The Ideal of Ballet Aesthetic. In: C. Steinberg, ed. *The Dance Anthology*. New York, NY: New York American Library, pp. 300–12.

Martin, R., 1990. Performance as Political Act: The Embodied Self. New York, NY: Bergin & Garvey.

Martin, R., 1992. Dance Ethnography and the Limits of Representation. *Social Text*, 33, pp. 102–23.

Martin, R., 1998. *Critical Moves: Dance Studies in Theory and Politics*. Durham, NC: Duke University Press.

Marx, K., [1910] 1969. *Theories of Surplus Value*. Translated by Renate Simpson. London: Lawrence and Wishart.

Marx, K., [1867] 1990. *Capital, Vol. 1*, translated by Ben Fowkes. New York, NY: Penguin.

Meglin, J., 2000. Review: *Dance in the City* by Helen Thomas. *Dance Research Journal*, 32(1), pp. 138–41.

Meinhof, U. and Triandafyllidou, A., 2006. Transcultural Europe: An Introduction to Cultural Policy in a Changing Europe. In: U. Meinhof and A. Triandafyllidou, eds. *Transcultural Europe: Cultural Policy in a Changing Europe*. Basingstoke: Palgrave MacMillan, pp. 3–24.

Mertes, T., 2003. Grass-Roots Globalism. In: G. Balakrishnan, ed. *Debating Empire*. London; New York, NY: Verso, pp. 144–55.

Morgenroth, J., 2004. *Speaking of Dance: Twelve Contemporary Choreographers on their Craft*. New York, NY; Abingdon: Routledge.

Morris, M., 2004. The Critique of Transcendence: Poststructuralism and the Political. *Political Theory*, 32(1), pp. 121–32.

Bibliography

Morris, G., 2006. *A Game for Dancers. Performing Modernism in the Postwar Years, 1945-1960.* Middletown, CT: Wesleyan University Press.

Mostov, J., 2008. *Soft Borders: Rethinking Sovereignty and Democracy.* London; New York, NY: Palgrave Macmillan.

Mowitt, J., 2008. Spins. *Postmodern Culture*, 18(2), n.p.

Murdock, G., 2002. Back to Work. Cultural Labor in Altered Times. In: A. Beck, ed. *Cultural Work: Understanding Cultural Industries.* London: Routledge Harwood.

Murray, C., and Gollmitzer, M., 2012. Escaping the Precarity Trap: A Call for Creative Labour Policy. *International Journal of Cultural Policy*, 18(4), pp. 419-38.

Negri, A., 2008. *Empire and Beyond.* Translated by Ed Emery. Cambridge: Polity Press.

Nicholas, L., 2001. Fellow Travellers: Dance and British Cold War Politics in the Early 1950s. *Dance Research: The Journal of the Society for Dance Research*, 19(2), pp. 83-105.

Nikolais, A., 1966. No Man from Mars. In: S. J. Cohen, ed. *The Modern Dance: Seven Statements of Belief.* Middletown, CT: Wesleyan University Press, pp. 64-5.

Novak, D., 2007. Labor of Likeness: Photography and Labor in Marx's *Capital*. *Criticism*, 49(2), pp. 125-50.

Noverre, J., 1983. Letters on Dancing and Ballets. In: R. Copeland, and M. Cohen, eds. *What is Dance? Readings in Theory and Criticism.* Oxford: Oxford University Press, pp. 10-5.

Ochs, E. and Capps, L., 1996. Narrating the Self. *Annual Review of Anthropology*, 25, pp. 19-43.

Olsen, F., 1997. Feminism in Central and Eastern Europe: Risks and Possibilities of American Engagement. *The Yale Law Journal*, 106(7), pp. 2215-57.

Ong, A., 1999. *Flexible Citizenship: The Cultural Logics of Transnationality*. Durham, NC; London: Duke University Press.

Opetchevska-Tatarchevska, I., 2009. Dance Culture and Identity: The Folk Dance Scene in the Republic of Macedonia between 1975 and 2005. In: Ž. Trajanoski et al. *The Echo of the Nation*. Skopje: Templum.

Ortner, S., 1984. Theory in Anthropology since the Sixties. *Comparative Studies in Society and History*, 26(1), pp. 126-66.

Ousmanova, A., 2003. On the Ruins of Orthodox Marxism: Gender and Cultural Studies in Eastern Europe. *Studies in East European Thought*, 55(1), pp. 37-50.

Öztürkmen, A., 2001. Politics of National Dance in Turkey: A Historical Reappraisal. *Yearbook of Traditional Music*, 33, pp. 139-43.

Öztürkmen, A., 2003. Modern Dance 'Alla Turca': Transforming Ottoman Dance in Early Republican Turkey. *Dance Research Journal*, 35(1), pp. 38-60.

Palat, A., 2000. The Postcolonial Aura: Third World Criticism in the Age of Global Capitalism. *Journal of World History*, 11(1), pp. 159-62.

Pang, L., 2009. The Labor Factor in the Creative Economy. *Social Text*, 99, 27(2), pp. 55-76.

Performance Studies international. 2012. PSi #18 Performance :: Culture :: Industry. [Online]. Available at: http://www.psi-web.org/detail/posts/10900 [Accessed 12 November 2013].

Peter, A., 2005. Somaesthetic, Education, and the Art of Dance. *The Journal of Aesthetic Education*, 39(1), pp. 48-64.

'Peter'. Personal Interview. 25 Aug. 2008.

Phelan, P., 1993. *Unmarked: The Politics of Performance*. New York, NY: Routledge.

Bibliography

Potuoğlu-Cook, Ö., 2006. Beyond the Glitter: Belly Dance and Neoliberal Gentrification in Istanbul. *Cultural Anthropology*, 21(4), pp. 633–60.

Pouillaude, F., 2007. Scène and Contemporaneity. Translated by Noémie Solomon. *The Drama Review: TDR*, 51(2), pp. 124–35.

Prevots, N., 1998. *Dance for Export: Cultural Diplomacy and the Cold War*. Hanover, NH: University Press of New England.

Puchner, M., 2002. The Theater in Modernist Thought. *New Literary History*, 33(3), pp. 521–32.

Rabinbach, A., 1992. *The Human Motor: Energy, Fatigue, and the Origins of Modernity*. Berkeley, CA: University of California Press.

Radcliffe, C., and Angliss, S., 2012. Revolution: Challenging the Automaton: Repetitive Labour and Dance in the Industrial Workspace. *Performance Research*, 17(6), pp. 40–7.

Radel, N., 2001. The Transnational Ga(y)ze: Constructing the East European Object of Desire in Gay Film and Pornography after the Fall of the Wall. *Cinema Journal*, 41(1), pp. 40–62.

Rainer, Y., 1979. No To Spectacle. In: S. J. Cohen, ed. *Dance as a Theater Art: Source History from 1581 to the Present*. New York, NY: Dodd Mead Publishing.

Ramet, S. P. ed., 1999. *Gender Politics in the Western Balkans*. Pennsylvania, PA: Pennsylvania State University Press.

Rayner, A., 2002. Rude Mechanicals and the *Specters of Marx*. *Theatre Journal*, 54(4), pp. 535–54.

Resina, J., 2003. The Scale of the Nation in a Shrinking World. *Diacritics*, 33(3/4), pp. 46–74.

Ridout, N., and Schneider, R., 2012. Precarity and Performance: An Introduction. *TDR: The Drama Review*, 56(4), pp. 5–9.

Risner, D., 2002. Rehearsing Heterosexuality: "Unspoken" Truths in Dance Education. *Dance Research Journal*, 34(2), pp. 63–78.

Risner, D., 2009. *Stigma and Perseverance in the Lives of Boys Who Dance: An Empirical Study of Male Identities in Western Theatrical Dance Training*. Lewiston, NY: Edwin Mellen Press.

Roberts, J., 2007. *The Intangibilities of Form: Skill and Deskilling in Art After the Readymade*. London; New York, NY: Verso.

Robin-Challan, L., 1992. Social Conditions of Ballet Dancers at the Paris Opéra in the 19th Century. *Choreography and Dance*, 2(1), pp. 17–28.

Roy, S., 1997. Contemporary Indian Dance in the Western City. In: H. Thomas, ed. *Dance in the City*. Basingstoke: Macmillan, pp. 68–87.

Rowe, N., 2009. Post-Salvagism: Choreography and Its Discontents in the Occupied Palestinian Territories. *Dance Research Journal*, 41(1), pp. 45–68.

Rowell, B., 2009. Dance Analysis in a Postmodern Age: Integrating Theory and Practice. In: J. Butterworth and L. Wildschut, eds. *Contemporary Choreography – A Critical Reader*. London; New York, NY: Routledge, pp. 136–52.

Rueschemeyer, M., 1998. *Women in the Politics of Postcommunist Eastern Europe*. Armonk, NY: M.E. Sharpe.

Sadowski-Smith, C., 1999. Contesting Globalisms: The Transnationalization of U.S. Cultural Studies. *Postmodern Culture*, 10(1), no page.

Bibliography

Salazar Parreñas, R., 2001. *Servants of Globalization: Women, Migration and Domestic Work*. Stanford, CA: Stanford University Press.

'Samir'. Personal interview. 10 Apr. 2009.

Savigliano, M., 2009. Worlding Dance and Dancing Out There in the World. In: S. Foster, ed. *Worlding Dance*. Basingstoke: Palgrave Macmillan, pp. 163–91.

Sayers, L. A., 1997. Madame Smudge, Some Fossils, and Other Missing Links: Unearthing the Ballet Class. In: H. Thomas, ed. *Dance in the City*. Basingstoke: Macmillan, pp. 130–47.

Scarry, E., 1985. *The Body in Pain: The Making and Unmaking of the World*. New York, NY: Oxford University Press.

Schlemmer, O., 1990. *The Letters and Diaries of Oskar Schlemmer*. Evanston, IL: Northwestern University Press.

Scolieri, P., 2008. Global/Mobile: Re-orienting Dance and Migration Studies. *Dance Research Journal*, 40(2), pp. v–xx.

Scott, G., 1997. Banes and Carroll on Defining Dance. *Dance Research Journal*, 29(1), pp. 7–22.

Shamir, R., 2005. Without Borders? Notes on Globalization as a Mobility Regime. *Sociological Theory*, 23(2), pp. 197–217.

Shapiro, S., ed., 1998. *Dance, Power, Difference: Critical and Feminist Perspectives on Dance Education*. Champaign, IL: Human Kinetics.

Shay, A., 1999. Parallel Traditions: State Folk Dance Ensembles and Folk Dance in "The Field". *Dance Research Journal*, 31(1), pp. 29–56.

Shay, A. and Fisher, J., 2009. Introduction. In: A. Shay, and J. Fisher, eds. *When Men Dance. Choreographing masculinities across borders*. New York, NY: Oxford University Press, pp. 3–27.

Shay, A. and Sellers-Young, B., eds., 2005. *Belly Dance: Orientalism, Transnationalism, and Harem Fantasy*. Costa Mesa, CA: Mazda Publishers.

Shilling, C., 2004. Physical Capital and Situated Action: A New Direction for Corporeal Sociology. *British Journal of Sociology of Education*, 25(4), pp. 473–87.

Siegel, M., 1972. *At the Vanishing Point: A Critic Looks at Dance*. New York, NY: Saturday Review Press.

Simpson, P., 2004. 'Periphering Patriarchy?' Gender and Identity in Post-Soviet Art: A View From the West. *Oxford Art Journal*, 27(3), pp. 389–415.

Smith, M. and Favell, A. eds., 2006. *The Human Face of Global Mobility: International Highly Skilled Migration in Europe, North America and the Asia-Pacific*. New Brunswick, NY: Transaction Publishers.

Spångberg, M., 2006. The Doing of Research. In: M. Hochmuth, K. Kruschkova, and G. Schöllhammer, eds. *It Takes Place When it Doesn't. On Dance and Performance Since 1989*. Frankfurt am Main: Revolver, pp. 59–73.

Sparshott, F., 1982. Why Do Philosophers Neglect the Aesthetic of the Dance? *Dance Research Journal*, 15(1), pp. 5–30.

Stinson, S., Blumenfield-Jones, D., and van Dyke, J., 1990. Voices of Young Women Dance Students: An Interpretive Study of Meaning in Dance. *Dance Research Journal*, 22(2), pp. 13–22.

Stoeltje, B., Fox, C., and Olbrys, S., 1999. The Self in the "Fieldwork": A Methodological Concern. *The Journal of American Folklore*, 112(444), pp. 158–82.

Stoneley, P., 2007. *A Queer History of the Ballet*. London: Routledge.

Summers-Bremner, E., 2000. Reading Irigaray, Dancing. *Hypatia*, 15(1), pp. 90–124.

Bibliography

Sussmann, L., 1990. Recruitment Patterns: Their Impact on Ballet and Modern Dance. *Dance Research Journal*, 22(1), pp. 21–8.

Šuvaković, M., 2010. Discourses and Dance: An Introduction to the Analysis of the Resistance of Philosophy and Theory to Dance. *TKH – Journal for Performing Arts Theory*, 18, pp. 10–24.

Tanurovska, B., 2007. *EU Cultural Policies in the Balkans*. MA Dissertation, University of Belgrade.

Terry, D. P., 2013. Showing Our Work. *Text and Performance Quarterly*, 33(3), pp. 223–4.

Thomas, H. ed., 1993. *Dance, Gender and Culture*. Basingstoke: Palgrave Macmillan.

Thomas, H., 1996. Do You Want to Join the Dance? Postmodernism/Poststructuralism, the Body, and Dance. In: G. Morris, ed. *Moving Words: Re-writing Dance*. London: Routledge, pp. 63–87.

Thomas, H., 2003. *The Body, Dance, and Cultural Theory*. Basingstoke: Palgrave Macmillan.

Thomas, H., 2004. Reconstruction and Dance as Embodied Textual Practice. In: A. Carter, ed. *Rethinking Dance History: A Reader*. London: Routledge, pp. 32–46.

Todorova, M., 1997. *Imagining the Balkans*. New York, NY: Oxford University Press.

True, J., 2003. *Gender, Globalization, and Postsocialism: The Czech Republic After Communism*. New York, NY: Columbia University Press.

Tsianos, V. and Papadopoulos, D., 2006. Who's Afraid of Immaterial Workers? Embodies Capitalism, Precarity, Imperceptibility. Available at www.preclab.net/text/06-tsianospapado-precarity.pdf. [Accessed 25 November 2009].

Tucker, R., 1980. *The Marx-Engels Reader.* (2nd ed.). New York, NY: W. W. Norton.

Unruh, V., 2012. 'Compañero, Respect Your Vacation!': Improvisations for a Workaday Crisis. *PMLA*, 127(4), pp. 731–50.

Verdery, K., 1996. *What Was Socialism, and What Comes Next?* Princeton, NJ: Princeton University Press.

Virno, P., 2003. *A Grammar of the Multitude: For an Analysis of Contemporary Forms of Life.* Translated by Isabella Bertoletti, James Cascaito, and Andrea Casson. Cambridge, MA; London: Semiotext(e).

Von Oppen, K., 2006. Imagining the Balkans, Imagining Germany: Intellectual Journeys in the Former Yugoslavia in the 1990s. *The German Quarterly*, 79(2), pp. 192–210.

Vujanović, A., 2007. Not Quite—Not Right Eastern Western Dance. Available at http://www.old.tkh-generator.net/sr/openedsource/not-quite-not-right-eastern-western-dance [Accessed 2 December 2013].

Wainwright, S. and Turner, B., 2004. Epiphanies of Embodiment: Injury, Identity, and the Balletic Body. *Qualitative Research*, 4(3), pp. 311–37.

Wendling, A., 2009. *Karl Marx on Technology and Alienation.* Basingstoke: Palgrave Macmillan.

Wikström, J., 2012. Practice Comes Before Labour: An Attempt to Read Performance Through Marx's Notion of Practice. *Performance Research*, 17(6), pp. 22–7.

Wolff, L., 1994. *Inventing Eastern Europe.* Stanford, CA: Stanford University Press.

Wood, E. M., 2003. A Manifesto for Global Capitalism? In: G. Balakrishnan, ed. *Debating Empire.* London; New York, NY: Verso, pp. 61–83.

Bibliography

Wulff, H., 1998. *Ballet Across Borders – Career and Culture in the World of Dancers*. Oxford; New York, NY: Berg.

Žižek, S., 1997. *The Abyss of Freedom/Ages of the World*. Ann Arbor, MI: University of Michigan Press.

Žižek, S., 2004. *Organs without Bodies: Deleuze and Consequences*. New York, NY; London: Routledge.

INDEX

aesthetic(s): 17, 26, 28, 30, 36, 40, 47–8, 62, 73, 80, 83, 84, 87, 110, 121, 143, 150, 161, 183, 188
anthropology: 7, 10, 54, 67– 8, 178, 182
artifice: 158–9

backstage economies: 48, 180, 191
ballet: 13, 15–16, 21, 49, 63, 93–5, 97, 111, 149, 152–4, 156–7, 159
biopolitics: 35–6, 82
biopower: 35– 6
body: 10–11, 14, 17–18, 20, 29, 72, 74, 94, 140, 149–50, 151, 152, 154, 158, 159, 162, 167, 181
borders: 37, 39–40, 43, 46, 52, 54, 65, 89–90, 134, 171, 178
Burt (Ramsay): 28–9, 74, 75–6, 87, 91–2, 94–5, 97, 100, 112, 182

capitalism: 23, 33, 35, 79, 80–1, 86, 87, 88, 133, 134, 143, 144, 151, 163–4, 167, 168, 169, 170, 177
community: 49, 50, 139, 166, 171, 172, 174, 191
contemporary dance: 2, 61–6, 71, 84, 89, 155, 157, 160, 163, 183, 185, 191
contemporary dancers: 9, 14, 156, 160, 165
creativity: 57, 63, 66, 82, 86, 89, 114–15, 119, 151, 160, 167
culture: 4, 14, 20, 22–4, 38, 42, 56, 57, 67, 86, 95, 134, 172, 180, 183–4

dance studies: 3, 4, 5, 6, 10–12, 16, 22, 25, 29, 30, 49, 71, 78, 171, 181, 182, 183, 184–5
dance technique: 2, 13–15, 17, 21, 63, 88, 133, 149, 150, 154, 155, 165, 167, 188
D'Andrea (Anthony): 88, 90, 137, 171, 178–9
Desmond (Jane): 3–4, 10–11, 29, 92, 182

Index

difference(s) 5, 39, 43, 48, 59, 66, 74–5, 87, 112, 123, 134–6, 180–2

Eastern Europe: 3, 7–8, 22–5, 40, 44–6, 52–3, 55, 62, 64, 125, 180
economy: 9, 33, 34, 38, 53, 57, 79–80, 84–5, 141–2, 154, 174, 183, 187, 188
empire: 33–4, 37, 38, 39, 134–6, 138, 139, 164, 168
European Union: 51
exotic: 1, 7, 65–6, 96

female dancers: 74, 75, 94, 98–9, 105, 111, 123
feminism: 10, 28, 45
folk dance: 73, 110, 122–3, 124
former Yugoslavia: 40, 61, 65–6, 123, 125, 138, 180

Gard (Michael): 69, 71, 76, 77–9, 92, 96, 98–100, 102–3, 107–9, 112, 118, 119, 124
gender: 6, 29, 30, 44–6, 48, 49, 55, 74, 75, 77, 93, 95, 96, 97, 99, 123–5, 135, 153–4, 180
globalization: 4, 6, 24, 37–9, 46, 54, 89, 133, 138, 170–2, 174, 175, 180, 181, 182, 185

Hamera (Judith): 2, 13, 40, 47, 93, 133, 154, 172, 188
Hardt and Negri: 33–7, 38, 72, 80, 89, 90, 133–6, 138–9, 165, 168, 169
hybridity: 34, 38, 42–4

immaterial labour: 36–7, 80, 83, 89, 133–5, 137–9, 169
international: 6, 59, 62, 64, 69, 137, 142, 175, 187

jobs: 8, 59, 80, 178

Kunst (Bojana): 2, 32, 37, 64–6, 171, 183, 186, 187

219

labour: 19, 57, 71–3, 79, 81, 82, 84, 85, 87, 144, 148–50, 154, 158, 166, 167, 170, 171, 186
local: 1, 2, 55, 59, 62, 64, 83, 170, 175–6, 177–8, 181, 188
Lepecki (Andre): 11, 16, 27, 30, 31–5, 81, 84, 143, 152, 183

Macedonia: 6, 60, 67, 68, 137, 138, 142
male dancers: 6, 45, 67–8, 74–7, 91–3, 94–8, 103, 110, 118, 125
Marx (Karl): 19–20, 133, 140–1, 143–5, 146–7, 151, 156–9, 163, 164–5
masculinity: 6, 45, 49, 69, 75–6, 78, 100, 112–14, 122, 124, 125–6
Middle East: 93, 99, 100, 104, 122, 125
mobility: 24, 37–9, 48, 49, 88, 105, 133, 137–9, 141, 163, 171, 172, 173, 175, 179–80
modernity: 10, 20, 32–3, 38, 61, 79, 80, 134, 164
movement (physical): 11, 14, 19–20, 22, 26, 27, 32, 62–3, 78, 88, 102, 110, 140, 152, 161, 172, 183
multitude: 134–7, 145, 168

national: 23, 40, 43, 45, 48, 51, 63, 70, 72, 88, 116, 178, 189
nation-state(s): 2, 43, 138, 140, 141, 142, 168–9

performance: 11, 26, 47, 48, 54–5, 81, 143, 144, 146, 150, 151, 170, 173, 182, 183, 186, 188, 191
philosophy: 28–31, 32, 178, 183
postmodernism: 10, 22–6, 28, 36
postsocialism: 42, 49, 54–5, 107
poststructuralism: 10, 16, 27, 28, 29, 150, 165
power: 18, 46, 54–5, 61, 68, 73, 77, 78, 89, 91–3, 97, 123, 139, 140–1, 148, 149–50, 158
precarious: 41, 42, 84, 172, 179, 188
production(s): 11, 17, 20, 31–3, 35–6, 38, 44, 80, 81, 143–5, 164–6, 169, 182

professional: 7, 40, 48, 57, 88, 92, 94–6, 98, 105, 123–4, 133, 134, 170, 172–3, 179
projects: 8–9, 51, 59, 62, 81, 82, 137, 168
representation: 11, 29, 41, 42, 44, 74, 76, 91, 92, 96, 123, 134, 143, 147, 149, 153

Romania: 6, 60, 67, 68, 108, 110, 112, 123, 137, 162

Serbia: 1, 6, 55, 58–64, 67, 68, 112, 137–8, 141, 174, 189
slow death: 189–91
sexuality (homo/hetero): 18, 55, 70, 75–7, 92, 94–5, 96, 99, 103, 104, 105, 112, 122, 123, 124
socialism: 2, 41, 46, 49, 52, 65, 100, 123–5, 138, 139, 180, 191
South East Europe: 2–3, 7, 8, 41, 60, 62, 66, 78, 89, 90, 93, 122, 124, 125, 135, 136, 138, 141, 179–80
sport: 56, 75, 96, 110, 118, 119, 156

threat: 40, 57, 89, 104, 174, 184, 188
transnational: 1, 38, 133, 139, 171, 177, 179, 182
travelling: 52, 133, 138
Tsianos and Papadopoulos: 140, 169
Turkey: 6, 45, 59, 60, 63, 67, 100, 105, 106, 124

virtuosic: 96, 144, 146, 167

war: 7–8, 22–4, 40, 51, 65–6, 79, 110, 114, 116–7, 125, 138, 152, 172, 180, 190